Probability models for data

The School Mathematics Project

CAMBRIDGE
UNIVERSITY PRESS

Main authors   Chris Belsom
                    Robert Black
                    David Cundy
                    Chris Little
                    Jane Southern
                    Fiona McGill

Team leader   Chris Belsom

Project director   Stan Dolan

The authors would like to give special thanks to Ann White for her help in producing
the trial edition and in preparing this book for publication.

The publishers would like to thank the following for supplying photographs:

front cover – Tick Ahearn.

Cartoons by Tony Hall

Published by the Press Syndicate of the University of Cambridge
The Pitt Building, Trumpington Street, Cambridge CB2 1RP
40 West 20th Street, New York, NY 10011–4211, USA
10 Stamford Road, Oakleigh, Melbourne 3166, Australia

First published 1992
Reprinted 1995

Produced by Gecko Limited, Bicester, Oxon.

Cover design by Iguana Creative Design

Printed in Great Britain at the University Press, Cambridge

British Library cataloguing in publication data

A catalogue record for this book is available from the British Library.

ISBN 0 521 40893 8 paperback

Contents

1 Models for data

1.1 Deterministic and probabilistic models

Some mathematical models are **deterministic** in nature. They provide exact information which can be used to predict future behaviour. For example, the path of a cricket ball can be modelled by equations of motion based on the laws of Newtonian mechanics. Various assumptions will be made. For example, you can treat the ball as a particle and so ignore spin; you can ignore frictional forces, or perhaps model them in some way (for example, as being proportional to the speed of the ball); and so on. Once the assumptions are made clear, however, the equation of motion which is produced by the mathematical model can be used to predict such things as time of flight, maximum height and range.

The Newton model of the solar system is regarded as a good model because predictions of events such as eclipses can be made with such accuracy. The 'goodness of fit' of any model can be assessed by considering how well the predictions fit in with actual events.

Statistical data are not deterministic in nature, but are subject to random variation so that you cannot predict future values with certainty. However, one of the themes of the unit *Living with uncertainty* was that long-term relative frequencies of events closely match predictable patterns, i.e. there is 'order from chaos'.

Although the path a ball takes through a binostat is unpredictable, when the experiment is repeated with a large number of balls, the relative frequencies of the balls exhibit a pattern which can be modelled mathematically.

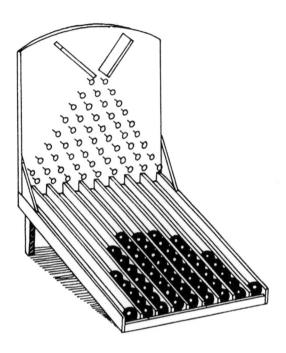

Although the values of statistical data can never be predicted with certainty, you can model relative frequencies with probabilities. You can then use the resulting **probability models** to make predictions and inferences. These will not have the exactness of a deterministic model, but their degree of uncertainty can be measured.

Which of the following situations are more likely to be successfully modelled with a deterministic mathematical model and which with a probabilistic mathematical model?

(a) the number of matches in a matchbox

(b) the amount the pound in your pocket will be worth in five years' time

(c) the flight of a space probe to the planet Mars

(d) the result of the next general election

(e) the rate of a nuclear reaction

(f) whether a new baby is a boy or a girl

1.2 Observed and expected frequencies

It is relatively easy to evaluate the appropriateness of a deterministic model: you can see if its predictions turn out to be true! With a probabilistic model, this is not so easy since it deals with uncertainties.

Suppose Mrs Bell has five daughters and is expecting a sixth child. She might predict from her experiences so far that the next one will also be a daughter. On the other hand, she sees roughly equal numbers of men and women walking the streets, and this might suggest that there is an equal chance of her next child being a boy or a girl.

(a) Are babies equally likely to be male or female?

Do you think that the sex of a first child affects that of a second? How could you find out?

(b) The following table of data concerns 100 families.

	Boy first	Girl first
Boy second	31	21
Girl second	22	26

Do these data affect your answers to (a)?

Provided you make a number of assumptions, you can **model** the situation considered in the discussion point. Suppose that:

● a baby is equally likely to be a boy or girl:

● the sex of the second child is independent of the first.

> Using these assumptions, show that the probability of each of the events (boy first, boy second), (boy first, girl second), (girl first, girl second) and (girl first, boy second) is 0.25.

Once you have established the probability model above, you can deduce the **expected frequencies** for each of the events by multiplying the probabilities (0.25 in each case) by the total number of families (100).

	Boy first	Girl first
Boy second	25	25
Girl second	25	25

Notice that these frequencies are 'expected' in the sense that they are predicted by the probability model. They are what you might 'expect' the frequencies observed to be 'close to', although you would certainly not expect to get these exact values. (The probability of obtaining any particular set of frequencies is very small.)

The closer the 'observed frequencies' of the data are to the 'expected frequencies' of the probability model, the more likely it is that the assumptions of the model are correct.

TASKSHEET 1 — Random numbers (page 11)

EXAMPLE 1

Two dice are thrown and the positive difference between their scores recorded. Calculate the expected frequencies for the difference in 600 such throws.

SOLUTION

The table lists all the possible number pairs and the difference each produces.

		First die					
		1	2	3	4	5	6
	1	0	1	2	3	4	5
	2	1	0	1	2	3	4
Second	3	2	1	0	1	2	3
die	4	3	2	1	0	1	2
	5	4	3	2	1	0	1
	6	5	4	3	2	1	0

From this table, you can count the number of ways differences can occur and hence obtain the associated probabilities as shown in the next table.

Difference	0	1	2	3	4	5
Number of ways	6	10	8	6	4	2
Probability	$\frac{3}{18}$	$\frac{5}{18}$	$\frac{4}{18}$	$\frac{3}{18}$	$\frac{2}{18}$	$\frac{1}{18}$
Expected frequency	100	167	133	100	67	33

$\frac{3}{18} \times 600$ = expected frequency
= 100

Three coins were tossed 800 times and the number of heads recorded. The following data were obtained:

Number of heads	0	1	2	3
Frequency	78	255	341	126

Construct a probability model for this situation and calculate the expected frequencies.

1.3 How good is the model?

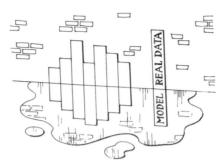

Suppose you have proposed a probability model and deduced expected frequencies. You could compare these with observed data. But how close should you **'expect'** these to be? How 'good' is the fit?

A measure of 'goodness of fit' which will give some idea of how far the observed frequencies are from the expected frequencies, and whether the discrepancy is 'reasonable', is introduced on tasksheet 2.

TASKSHEET 2 – Measuring bias (page 12)

A suitable measure of goodness of fit is obtained by dividing the square of the difference between each observed and expected frequency by the expected frequency and then adding together the results.

> The 'goodness of fit' test statistic, X^2, is defined by:
>
> $$X^2 = \sum \frac{(O - E)^2}{E}$$
>
> O stands for 'Observed frequency'
> E stands for 'Expected frequency'

EXERCISE 1

1 (a) Calculate X^2 for the following birth data:

	Boy first	Girl first
Boy second	31	21
Girl second	22	26

(i) assuming P(boy) = P(girl) = 0.5;

(ii) assuming P(boy) = 0.513.

(b) Which model in (a) gives the closer fit?

2 Before she can start 'snakes and ladders', Sonja needs to throw a six. She thinks she is unlucky at this and even goes to the trouble of recording some data.

Number of throws before a six	1	2	3	4	5	6 or more	
Frequency	25	24	23	22	15	91	Total = 200

Let N be the number of throws before a six is obtained.

(a) Using a tree diagram or otherwise, show that:

(i) $P(N = 1) = \frac{1}{6}$

(ii) $P(N = 2) = (\frac{1}{6})(\frac{5}{6})$

(iii) $P(N = 3) = (\frac{1}{6})(\frac{5}{6})^2$

(b) Deduce the probability distribution for N and calculate the expected frequencies corresponding to the observed frequencies.

(c) Calculate X^2 for the given data.

3 At the local library, the number of books loaned on each day of a particular week were:

Monday	Tuesday	Wednesday	Thursday	Friday	Saturday
200	290	250	285	265	270

Calculate X^2 on the basis of a probability model which assumes that all books are equally likely to be borrowed on any day.

After working through this chapter you should:

1 understand the difference between a deterministic and a probabilistic model and know when each is appropriate;

2 understand the terms observed and expected frequencies, and calculate expected frequencies from a probability model;

3 be able to calculate the 'goodness of fit' statistic:

$$X^2 = \sum \frac{(O - E)^2}{E}$$

Random numbers

1 (a) As quickly as you can, write down a sequence of zeros and ones which you believe to be random. Record 101 numbers.

(b) Consider the string of numbers in pairs and record the observed frequencies of the four pairs (0, 0), (0, 1), (1, 0) and (1, 1) in your sequence. For example, the sequence:

    0 1 0 0 1 0

generates the pairs (0, 1), (1, 0), (0, 0), (0, 1) and (1, 0) and gives:

Pair	(0, 0)	(0, 1)	(1, 0)	(1, 1)
Frequency	1	2	2	0

(c) Assuming the sequence was random, what are the probabilities of obtaining each of the number pairs (0, 0), (1, 0), (0, 1) and (1, 1)? Hence write down the expected frequencies of each pair in a sequence of 101 zeros and ones at random.

(d) Compare the observed and the expected frequencies. Do you think your sequence **is** a random sequence?

In this course, statistical problems have often been simulated using the random number generator on a computer or calculator. Doing this has begged the question of whether the numbers generated are truly random.

2 (a) Repeat question 1 using the random number facility on your calculator. You will need to consider how to use the random number generated to produce a sequence of zeros and ones. One way of doing this would be to treat each digit as a member of the sequence, counting 0–4 as a zero, and 5–9 as a one.

(b) (i) Is the calculator 'better' than you are at generating random sequences?

(ii) How could you tell?

Measuring bias

If you wanted to check whether a die was biased towards scoring a six or a one, you could throw it, for example 1200 times, and record the number of ones, sixes and other scores.

Suppose you obtained the results below for dice A, B, C and D (which was thrown only 600 times):

Die A	1	6	Other
Observed	182	238	780
Expected	200	200	800

Die B	1	6	Other
Observed	201	199	800
Expected	200	200	800

Die C	1	6	Other
Observed	220	218	762
Expected	200	200	800

Die D	1	6	Other
Observed	120	118	362
Expected	100	100	400

1 Explain why the expected frequencies for an unbiased die would be 200 ones, 200 sixes and 800 other scores.

2 Which of the dice A, B, C and D appear to be biased?

A measure of 'goodness of fit' is needed which confirms an intuitive idea of how biased the dice appear to be.

3   One possibility would be to calculate the deviation ($+$ or $-$) between **observed** and **expected** frequency for each category, or cell, and then sum these.

   (a) Calculate this for die A.

   (b) Why is it not a satisfactory measure?

4   To improve the measure used in question 3, you could square the deviations, then add. You could write this measure as:

$$\Sigma(\text{observed} - \text{expected})^2$$

where the sum is across all the categories or cells.

   (a) Calculate $\Sigma(\text{observed} - \text{expected})^2$ for each die.

   (b) Compare the results for die C and die D. Why is this measure not satisfactory?

   (c) Compare the results for die A and die C. Why is this measure not satisfactory?

A better measure is to divide the squared differences in each cell by the expected frequency. This gives the statistic:

$$\Sigma \frac{(\text{observed} - \text{expected})^2}{\text{expected}}$$

For die A, this works out as:

$$\frac{(182 - 200)^2}{200} + \frac{(238 - 200)^2}{200} + \frac{(780 - 800)^2}{800} = 9.34$$

This 'goodness of fit' statistic is usually denoted by X^2. (The reason for this choice of symbol will become apparent later.)

5   (a) Calculate X^2 for the dice B, C and D.

   (b) List all four dice in order of increasing value of X^2.

The larger the value of X^2 obtained, the further the observed frequencies deviate from the expected frequencies for an unbiased die, and hence the more likely it is that the die is biased.

The X^2 results for the dice A, B, C and D should confirm your intuition about which are more likely to be biased.

2 The chi-squared test

2.1 The distribution of X^2

In chapter 1, you met a statistic, X^2, for measuring the 'goodness of fit' of a probability model when applied to data.

$$X^2 = \sum \frac{(O - E)^2}{E}$$
O stands for observed frequency
E stands for expected frequency

Thus for die A, assuming it is unbiased, you calculated X^2 as 9.34 for the following data:

Die A	1	6	Other
Observed	182	238	780
Expected	200	200	800

Similarly, for dice B, C and D, the X^2 values were 0.01, 5.42 and 10.85 respectively. These values suggest that die D is the most likely to be biased, whereas the results for die B seem almost too good to be true!

The statistics program, *Chi-squared*, simulates the throwing of an unbiased die up to 1200 times. It records the number of ones, sixes and other values and then calculates the value of X^2 for each sample of throws. The program takes a long time to run if the number of throws is large and it is therefore easier to illustrate its use with, for example, only 60 throws.

Die E	1	6	Other	
Observed	18	13	29	$X^2 \approx 10.3$
Expected	10	10	40	

(a) How could you use the program to decide if a die is unbiased?

(b) Use the program to help you decide how likely it is that die E is biased.

The distribution of X^2 can be modelled mathematically. It can be approximated by one of a family of distributions known as the chi-squared (χ^2) distributions, written $\chi^2(1)$, $\chi^2(2)$, $\chi^2(3)$ and so on. (χ (chi) is the Greek letter X: hence the use of X^2 in the 'goodness of fit' statistic.)

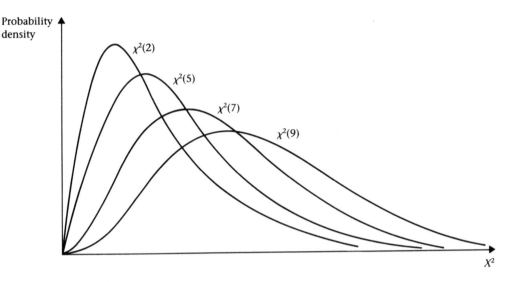

Probability density

X^2

The n of $\chi^2(n)$ is known as the number of **degrees of freedom** and is often denoted by the greek letter ν (nu). For die D, for example:

Score	1	6	Other
Frequency	120	118	362

Once the frequencies for score 1 and score 6 are known, the frequency of the other scores is fixed as $600 - (120 + 118)$, so the relevant χ^2 distribution has two degrees of freedom.

The actual mathematical function for $\chi^2(n)$ is complicated. In practice, as in the case of the Normal distribution, all you need to know is how the area is distributed.

A typical table of χ^2 probabilities is illustrated.

p		.1	.05	.025	.01	.005	.001
$v =$	1	2.71	3.84	5.02	6.63	7.88	10.83
	2	4.61	5.99	7.38	9.21	10.60	13.81
	3	6.25	7.81	9.35	11.34	12.84	16.27
	4	7.78	9.49	11.14	13.28	14.86	18.47
	5	9.24	11.07	12.83	15.09	16.75	20.52
	6	10.64	12.59	14.45	16.81	18.55	22.46
	7	12.02	14.07	16.01	18.48	20.28	24.32
	8	13.36	15.51	17.53	20.09	21.95	26.12
	9	14.68	16.92	19.02	21.67	23.59	27.88
	10	15.99	18.31	20.48	23.21	25.19	29.59
	12	18.55	21.03	23.34	26.22	28.30	32.91
	14	21.06	23.68	26.12	29.14	31.32	36.12
	16	23.54	26.30	28.85	32.00	34.27	39.25
	18	25.99	28.87	31.53	34.81	37.16	42.31
	20	28.41	31.41	34.17	37.57	40.00	45.31
	25	34.38	37.65	40.65	44.31	46.93	52.62
	30	40.26	43.77	46.98	50.89	53.67	59.70
	40	51.81	55.76	59.34	63.69	66.77	73.40
	50	63.17	67.50	71.42	76.15	79.49	86.66
	60	74.40	79.08	83.30	88.38	91.95	99.61
	100	118.5	124.3	129.6	135.8	140.2	149.4

Joint Matriculation Board

The table shows, for any χ^2 function, the proportion of the area which lies to the right of certain values of X^2.

Graph of the χ^2 density function for $v = 12$

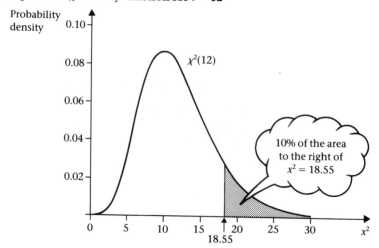

This means that the probability of obtaining a value of $\chi^2(12)$ greater that 18.55 is 0.1.

Find the value 18.55 in the table. Find also:

(a) the value of $\chi^2(12)$ which has 1% of the area to the right;

(b) the value of $\chi^2(5)$ which has 5% of the area to the right.

You are now in a position to make some judgement on each of the dice. For die A the observed data led to an X^2 value of 9.34. There are only two degrees of freedom, so consider $\chi^2(2)$.

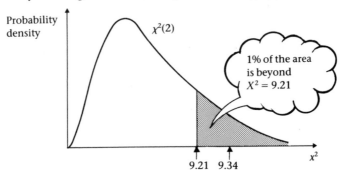

A value of X^2 greater than 9.21 would occur in fewer than 1% of cases. This suggests that the model used for die A (that of an unbiased die) is **not** a good fit to the real data. The difference between the expected and observed frequencies is high, and such a high value for X^2 would occur in fewer than 1% of cases by chance alone. There is strong evidence to suggest that A is biased.

Consider the other dice in the same way.

EXERCISE 1

Use a χ^2 probability table for the following questions.

1 X^2 has a χ^2 distribution with five degrees of freedom.

(a) What is the probability that X^2 is greater than 12.83?

(b) In what percentage of samples does X^2 exceed 11.07?

(c) For what proportion of samples is X^2 less than 0.831?

2 X^2 has a χ^2 distribution with ten degrees of freedom.

(a) X^2 exceeds the value a in 5% of samples. Find a.

(b) X^2 is less than b in 1% of samples. Find b.

(c) There is a 2.5% probability of X^2 exceeding the value c. Find c.

2.2 Testing a model

In a project to investigate the distribution of the number of girls in families, the following data were obtained for families having three children.

Number of girls	0	1	2	3	
Number of families	9	17	21	4	Total = 51 families

A binomial probability model, having $p = 0.5$ and $n = 3$, is proposed for the numbers of girls in families of size three. The model is used as a basis for calculating the **expected frequencies**.

$$P(2 \text{ girls}) = \binom{3}{2}\left(\frac{1}{2}\right)^2\left(\frac{1}{2}\right) = \frac{3}{8}$$

Number of girls	0	1	2	3
Probability	$\frac{1}{8}$	$\frac{3}{8}$	$\frac{3}{8}$	$\frac{1}{8}$
Expected frequency in 51 families	6.38	19.13	19.13	6.38

$\frac{1}{8} \times 51$

Confirm that the probability of one girl in a family of three is $\frac{3}{8}$ and that the expected frequency is 19.13.

Calculate X^2 for the data:

$$X^2 = \sum \frac{(O - E)^2}{E}$$

$$= \frac{(9 - 6.38)^2}{6.38} + \frac{(17 - 19.13)^2}{19.13} + \frac{(21 - 19.13)^2}{19.13} + \frac{(4 - 6.38)^2}{6.38}$$

$$= 2.38$$

There are four cells. In this case, the number of degrees of freedom is $4 - 1 = 3$. From tables of $\chi^2(3)$, the 5% (or 0.05) value of X^2 is 7.81. The value obtained (2.38) is certainly not above this value and so is not unusual. This suggests good agreement between the model and the real data. The result is said to be **not significant**.

If you obtain a value for X^2 greater than 7.81, then the difference between the values predicted by the model and those actually observed (the real data) would have been greater than would have been expected by chance variation alone. The model seems inappropriate for the data. In such a case, the result is **significant at the 5% level**.

A word of warning here – the χ^2 test as described above should only be used if the expected frequency of a cell is **more than 5**. Otherwise, groups/cells must be combined. The total frequency should also be **50 or more**.

EXERCISE 2

For all the probability models proposed in this exercise, assume that X^2 has a χ^2 distribution with $(c - 1)$ degrees of freedom, where c is the number of cells.

1 'Prison inmates are more violent during the hot summer months'. Test this statement, using the following data for a prison in Florida.

Month	Jan	Feb	Mar	Apr	May	Jun	Jul	Aug	Sep	Oct	Nov	Dec
Number of assaults	30	30	33	42	25	28	41	32	48	28	28	24

2 Six samples of 180 men under the age of forty were selected randomly from a large population to test the hypothesis that one-sixth of men have black hair. The numbers observed were 40, 35, 30, 30, 25 and 20. Is there evidence against the hypothesis?

3 According to Mendel's theory of genetics, the number of peas of a certain variety which fall into the classifications round and yellow, wrinkled and yellow, round and green, and wrinkled and green, should be in the ratio 9:3:3:1. Suppose that for 100 such peas, 55, 20, 16 and 9 were in these respective classes. Do these results agree with Mendelian theory?

4 Imported peaches come in boxes each holding six peaches. A batch of 100 boxes in a supermarket revealed the following distribution of imperfect fruit amongst the boxes.

Number of imperfect peaches in box	0	1	2	3	4	5	6
Frequency	50	25	14	8	2	1	0

Use the data to estimate the proportion of imperfect peaches. Use this to calculate the expected frequency of boxes out of 100 with 0, 1, 2, and 3 or more imperfect peaches. Then conduct a χ^2 goodness of fit test on these four cells, and test the model.

2.3 Calculating the degrees of freedom

The number of degrees of freedom is the number of **independent** cells used to calculate the value of X^2. This is equal to the number of cells minus the number of **constraints**. For example, in a die experiment where you record ones, sixes and other scores in 120 throws, you might obtain:

Score	1	6	Others	
Frequency	25	18	77	Total = 120

Here, there are three cells and one constraint (that the total is 120). Therefore there are $3 - 1 = 2$ degrees of freedom.

Further constraints on the observed frequencies are considered in the next tasksheet.

TASKSHEET 1 — Counting constraints (page 26)

Number of degrees of freedom	=	number of cells	−	number of constraints

Since the total frequency is fixed, this is always a constraint. In addition, each time the data are used to estimate a parameter for the model (such as p in the binomial model), this adds another constraint and reduces the number of degrees of freedom by one. For example, suppose you had collected the following data on the number of girls in 100 families of size four.

Number of girls	0	1	2	3	4	
Number of families	5	24	37	30	4	Total = 100

If you were to compare these data with the frequencies expected on the basis of using $B(4, \frac{1}{2})$ for the number of girls in each family, then the number of degrees of freedom (ν) is:

Number of cells $-1 = 4$

If, instead, you were to use $B(4, p)$ with p calculated from the data as $\frac{204}{400} = 0.51$, then there would be the extra constraint that the mean of the model must equal the mean of the data and:

$\nu = 5 - 2 = 3$

2.4 Contingency tables

In the remainder of this unit, you will be looking at a range of probability models which can be used to model data. The χ^2 goodness of fit test can be used as a check to see if a model is appropriate, or to see if the assumptions behind a model are valid.

This section considers a particularly common and useful application of χ^2 which tests the **independence** of two characteristics.

Here are some data on voting intentions for a parish council election in a small rural community. They are classified according to the age of the voters. There were only two candidates, one Labour and one Conservative. 'Don't knows' were discounted.

	Age (years)				
	18–25	26–40	41–60	60+	Total
Will vote Labour	5	27	13	21	66
Will vote Conservative	14	35	47	56	152
Total	19	62	60	77	218

This sort of two-way table is called a **contingency table**.

Do these data suggest that there is a connection between age and voting intention? If there were no connection, what would you expect the frequencies in each age category to be?

You can model this situation with the assumption that voting intention is unrelated to age. Under these circumstances, the total in each age category should vote in the same ratio as the total number of voters. You can then test the model using a χ^2 goodness of fit test.

TASKSHEET 2 – *Voting and age (page 27)*

You can generalise to find a rule for the number of degrees of freedom in this sort of test. The row and column totals are fixed in determining the model. Suppose you had a four by five table:

Observed table of values

	A	B	C	D	E	Total
i						fixed
ii						fixed
iii						fixed
iv						fixed
Total	fixed	fixed	fixed	fixed	fixed	

(a) Why are there three free entries in each column, and four free entries in each row?

(b) For this table, there are $3 \times 4 = 12$ degrees of freedom. How many degrees of freedom are there for an m by n table?

The χ^2 distribution is used to test the calculated value of X^2 for the data. Conditions on its use are that the **expected frequency** of each cell must be five or more and that the **total frequency** should be at least 50. Under such conditions, χ^2 satisfactorily models the distribution of the difference measure, X^2. However, the approximation is less good when there is only one degree of freedom. This is always the case for 2×2 contingency tables. A correction to improve the fit, known as Yates's correction, is sometimes used to improve the situation. However, this correction will be ignored here.

EXAMPLE 1

In a trial, 120 out of 200 women can distinguish margarine from butter, whereas 108 out of 200 men can tell the difference. Does this trial provide evidence of a gender-related difference in taste discrimination?

SOLUTION

The data can be expressed in a 2 × 2 contingency table.

	Men	Women	Total
Can tell	108	120	228
Cannot tell	92	80	172
Total	200	200	400

A model based on the assumption that there is no difference in the ability of men and women to distinguish between butter and margarine would lead to the following expected frequencies:

	Men	Women	
Can tell	114	114	228
Cannot tell	86	86	172
Total	200	200	400

$\frac{228}{400}$ can tell the difference. You would expect that $\frac{228}{400}$ of the 200 women to be able to do so, i.e. $\frac{228}{400} \times 200 = 114$

Calculating the difference measure,

$$X^2 = \sum \frac{(O-E)^2}{E}$$

$$X^2 = \frac{(108-114)^2}{114} + \frac{(120-114)^2}{114} + \frac{(92-86)^2}{86} + \frac{(80-86)^2}{86}$$

$X^2 = 1.47$ with one degree of freedom

As this value does not exceed the $\chi^2(1)$ value of 2.71, then the difference between the observed values and those of the model is **not** significant.

There is no evidence (from the data) that ability to distinguish between margarine and butter is gender-related.

EXERCISE 3

1 The following data compare performances of candidates in the sociology honours degree at two colleges.

	Grade				
	1	2	3	4	Total
College A	6	66	114	56	242
College B	5	40	86	49	180

Is there a significant difference in grades awarded?

2 In a hospital survey, staff were asked whether they were satisfied or dissatisfied in their work. Results were as follows:

	Satisfied	Not satisfied	Total
Doctors	50	20	70
Nurses	30	30	60
Ancillary staff	12	48	60
Total	92	98	190

What evidence do these data provide that job satisfaction is related to the type of job?

3 In a clinical trial of a drug for arthritis, 200 patients received treatment with the drug, and a control group of 200 received treatment with a seemingly identical placebo (which is non-active). After a period of time, patients were asked if their condition had improved. The results were as follows:

	Drug	Placebo
Improved	119	72
Not improved	81	128

Conduct a χ^2 test to decide if these results give evidence (significant at the 5% level) that the drug is effective in improving the condition.

After working through this chapter you should:

1 know that the goodness of fit statistic X^2 has a distribution which can be modelled by one of the chi-squared functions;

2 know the conditions under which the χ^2 test may be applied;

3 know how to work out areas under the χ^2 distribution using probability tables, and interpret these results in terms of probability;

4 understand what is meant by significance level as applied to problems involving fitting probability models;

5 be able to apply a χ^2 goodness of fit test to test probability models for data, including contingency tables;

6 know how to work out the number of degrees of freedom by considering the number of constraints on the observed frequencies.

Counting constraints

The following data for the distribution of girls in 51 families of three children were considered earlier.

Number of girls	0	1	2	3
Number of families	9	17	21	4

If you assume that boys and girls are equally likely to be born ($p = 0.5$) then you see that the binomial model gives a value of $X^2 = 2.38$.

Instead, you could **use the data** to estimate the proportion of girls and then model the data with a binomial distribution using this estimate for p.

1 (a) Show that the total number of girls in this sample is 71.

   (b) Show that the proportion of girls in the sample is 0.464.

   (c) Using this value as an estimate of p, the proportion of girls in the population, complete the following binomial probability distribution and the expected frequencies.

Number of girls per family	0	1	2	3
Probability	0.154	0.400		
Expected frequency	7.85	20.4		

2 (a) Calculate the value of X^2 for the model above.

   (b) Confirm that this is lower than the value obtained by taking $p = 0.5$. Why do you think this is?

There is now an extra constraint on the observed frequencies. Not only does the total observed frequency have to be 51; in addition, the total number of girls must be 71, to give the estimated probability of 0.464.

3 Given these two constraints and the first two observed frequencies of 9 and 17, deduce that the other two observed frequencies **must** be 21 and 4 respectively.

By estimating the proportion (p) from the observed frequencies, an extra constraint has been added to the observed frequencies. The number of degrees of freedom is therefore reduced by one. There are four cells and two constraints, giving $4 - 2 = 2$ degrees of freedom. The correct distribution for X^2 in this case is $\chi^2(2)$.

Voting and age

Suppose a contingency table of age against voting intention is as follows:

	Age in years				
	18–25	26–40	41–60	60+	Total
Will vote Labour	5	27	13	21	66
Will vote Conservative	14	35	47	56	152
Total	19	62	60	77	218

A total of 66 out of 218 intend to vote Labour and 152 out of 218 intend to vote Conservative. Assuming that age does not affect voting intention, you would expect the following frequencies in the 18–25 category. Note that $0.303 \approx \frac{66}{218}$ and $0.697 \approx \frac{152}{218}$.

Will vote Labour	$19 \times 0.303 = 5.8$
Will vote Conservative	$19 \times 0.697 = 13.2$
Total	19

1 Calculate expected frequencies for the remaining age categories and hence complete the following table of **expected frequencies**.

	18–25	26–40	41–60	60+	Total
Will vote Labour	5.8				66
Will vote Conservative	13.2				152
Total	19	62	60	77	218

2 Calculate $X^2 = \sum \dfrac{(O-E)^2}{E}$ for the eight cells of the table.

In determining the expected frequencies, both the row totals (to determine the overall proportion of Labour/Conservative voters) and the column totals (to calculate the expected frequencies in each age category) have been used. So these are fixed constraints on the **observed frequencies** in the table:

	18–25	26–40	41–60	60+	Total
Will vote Labour					66
Will vote Conservative					152
Total	19	62	60	77	218

3 For this case, once three observed frequencies are known, the others are determined by the row and column totals. Therefore, $\nu = 3$.

Complete the χ^2 test and comment on whether voting intention is related to age.

3 Probability distributions for counting cases

3.1 Introduction

Most people's lives follow a fairly routine pattern. Chance events do affect this pattern. Nevertheless, an order emerges from the 'chaos' of random events.

Some of the emerging pattern may be modelled by random variables and the probability distributions which describe their behaviour. For example, the number of girls in a family with four children is a random variable, X, which can take any of the values $X = 0, 1, 2, 3$ or 4.

You should be aware that, with appropriate assumptions, X has a binomial probability distribution:

$$X \sim B(4, 0.5)$$

State the necessary assumptions.

In *Living with uncertainty*, you considered the binomial distribution in some detail and *The Normal distribution* was based entirely on one important probability distribution for a continuous random variable which is important for much of statistics.

Another type of distribution is the **uniform distribution**, in which a set of values (for example, the numbers 1, 2, 3, 4, 5, and 6 which are obtained when a die is thrown) occur with equal probability (namely $\frac{1}{6}$). If S is the random variable for the score on a die, you can express the probability distribution mathematically.

S is uniform on $(1, 2, 3, 4, 5, 6)$

$P(S = r) = \frac{1}{6}$ where $1 \leqslant r \leqslant 6$

For a general uniform distribution, show that:

$$P(X = r) = \frac{1}{k} \qquad \text{for } r = 1, 2, \ldots, k$$

3.2 The geometric distribution

All the distributions which will be considered in this chapter apply to random variables which count events and therefore take whole number values 0, 1, 2 and so on. The situations which they can be used to model will be compared and contrasted.

For example, one day a midwife delivers eight boys in a row before the first girl is born. How rare is this event?

First you must clearly define a random variable. In this case, let X be the number of boys born before the first girl.

 Why is the binomial distribution not a suitable model for the distribution of X?

 TASKSHEET 1 — It's a girl (page 38)

If the random variable X counts the number of **independent trials** before the occurrence of an event whose probability is p, then X has a geometric distribution.

The geometric distribution, abbreviated to G(p), is defined in the following way:

$$P(X = r) = q^{r-1}p \qquad \text{where } r = 1, 2, 3, \ldots$$

X can never equal 0. Why not?

EXAMPLE 1

To start a game of snakes and ladders, you need to throw a six. Calculate the probability that it takes more than six throws to get a six.

SOLUTION

Define the distribution

Let X be the number of throws before a six. Then $X \sim G(\frac{1}{6})$

$$
\begin{aligned}
P(X > 6) &= 1 - P(X \leqslant 6) \\
&= 1 - [P(X = 1) + P(X = 2) + \ldots + P(X = 6)] \\
&= 1 - [\tfrac{1}{6} + (\tfrac{5}{6})\tfrac{1}{6} + (\tfrac{5}{6})^2\tfrac{1}{6} + \ldots + (\tfrac{5}{6})^5\tfrac{1}{6}] \\
&= 0.335
\end{aligned}
$$

The probability that it takes more than six throws is 0.335.

The distribution of X is illustrated.

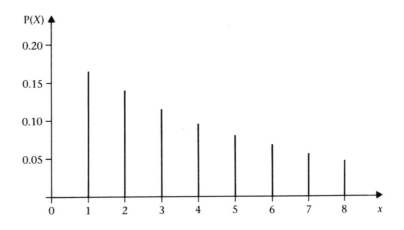

EXERCISE 1

1 X has a geometric distribution with $p = 0.2$. Calculate:

(a) $P(X = 3)$

(b) $P(X < 3)$

(c) $P(X \geqslant 3)$

2 I have a key ring on which there are four keys, all of the same type. To get into my office I select a key at random.

(a) If it is a wrong key then I choose another at random from the remaining three. Calculate the probability that I try:

(i) two keys;   (ii) all four keys.

(b) If, instead, I simply keep choosing at random from all four keys until I get the correct one, calculate the probability that I try:

    (i) two keys;   (ii) more than two keys.

(c) Which is the best strategy for getting into my room? Why?

3   Suppose that each time you take a driving test you have a probability of 0.4 of passing. What is the probability that you:

(a) pass the test on the third attempt;

(b) need at least six attempts to pass?

4   From a table of random numbers, what is the probability that:

(a) you select five digits and you still do not have a zero;

(b) you need to select more than twenty digits to obtain your first zero?

3.3 The binomial distribution revisited

On a particular morning, there are ten babies in the maternity ward at a local hospital. Only one of them is a boy. Just how likely an event is this?

(a) Identify the random variable and an appropriate binomial distribution to model it.

(b) Discuss the differences between the binomial and the geometric distributions by considering the conditions under which each applies.

To calculate binomial probabilities in *Living with uncertainty*, you used Pascal's triangle to work out $\binom{n}{r}$, the number of ways of choosing r objects from n. When n gets large, this is cumbersome. Even though you can use the Normal approximation to the binomial when n is large, the following formula for evaluating $\binom{n}{r}$ is useful.

$$\binom{n}{r} = \frac{n!}{r!(n-r)!} \qquad \text{where } n! = n(n-1)(n-2)\ldots 1 \\ \text{and} \quad 0! = 1$$

$\binom{n}{r}$ is sometimes written as ^nC_r or $_nC_r$.

If $X \sim B(n, p)$, then:

$$P(X = r) = \binom{n}{r} p^r q^{n-r} \qquad r = 0, 1, 2, \ldots, n$$

$$P(X = r) = \frac{n!}{r!(n-r)!}\, p^r q^{n-r}$$

Use the factorial form of the binomial distribution to find the probability of there being only one male baby in a group of ten.

EXAMPLE 2

Approximately 20% of the pupils at a primary school are vegetarians. Seven of the pupils are to visit another school and have lunch there. Calculate the probability that, in addition to normal requirements, the school will need to provide:

(a) three vegetarian lunches; (b) at least one vegetarian lunch.

SOLUTION

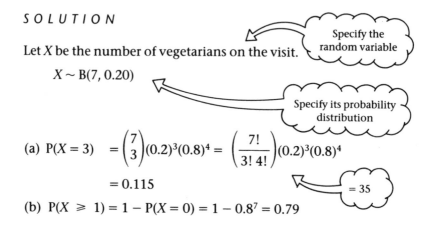

Let X be the number of vegetarians on the visit.

> Specify the random variable

$$X \sim B(7, 0.20)$$

> Specify its probability distribution

(a) $P(X = 3) = \binom{7}{3}(0.2)^3(0.8)^4 = \left(\dfrac{7!}{3!\,4!}\right)(0.2)^3(0.8)^4$

$$= 0.115$$

> $= 35$

(b) $P(X \geqslant 1) = 1 - P(X = 0) = 1 - 0.8^7 = 0.79$

 TASKSHEET 2E – *Programming the binomial (page 39)*

EXERCISE 2

1 In a series of five matches between two teams, calculate the probability that one team wins the toss:

(a) on exactly three occasions; (b) on three or more occasions.

2 If $X \sim B(8, \frac{2}{3})$, find the most likely value of X.

3 Six people, selected at random, sample two brands of orange squash, brands A and B. If five of them say they prefer brand B, do you think this is sufficient evidence for an advertiser to say, 'Most people prefer brand B.'? Explain.

4 In a test where there are only three alternatives to each of the twenty questions, a student randomly guesses each answer. If fifteen is the pass mark for the test, calculate the probability that he passes.

5E A coin is tossed eight times. What is the probability that there will be more tails on the first four throws than on the last four?

3.4 The Poisson distribution

A small company handles emergency medical deliveries by motor cycle. On average, it receives four delivery requests in a 12-hour period. When it gets more than four emergency requests, it has to pass on the work to another company. The company wishes to know the probability of this happening to enable them to evaluate their policy.

Let X be the number of emergency calls in a 12-hour period.

> What values can X take? Could the distribution of X be binomial, or geometric? What sort of shape do you think the graph of the distribution will take?

In order to find out the true probability distribution of X, you could try to stimulate the situation.

TASKSHEET 3 – Emergency deliveries (page 41)

The correct probability distribution for this type of situation is called the **Poisson distribution**, after the French statistician, Simeon Denis Poisson (1781–1840).

X is said to have a Poisson distribution with mean λ if:

$$P(X = r) = \frac{e^{-\lambda}\lambda^r}{r!} \qquad \text{for } r = 0, 1, 2, 3, \ldots$$

This is written as:

$$X \sim P(\lambda)$$

Poisson derived his probability distribution by considering what happens to the binomial distribution when n increases and np is kept fixed.

The mean of the binomial distribution $B(n, p)$ is np. As it is np that determines the particular Poisson distribution $P(\lambda)$, then it is likely that λ will be the mean of the Poisson. This result will be proved in the next chapter, which considers the means of the various distributions.

TASKSHEET 3E – *From binomial to Poisson (page 43)*

EXAMPLE 3

Cars arrive at a petrol station at an average rate of two cars every 10 minutes. For a given 10-minute period, calculate the probability that:

(a) exactly three cars arrive;   (b) two or more cars arrive.

SOLUTION

(a) Let X be the number of cars arriving in a 10-minute period.

$$X \sim P(\lambda = 2)$$

$$P(X = 3) \; = \; \frac{e^{-2}2^3}{3!}$$

$$= 0.180$$

Define its distribution

Define the random variable

(b) $P(X \geqslant 2) = 1 - P(X < 2)$
$$= 1 - [P(X = 0) + P(X = 1)]$$
$$= 1 - \left[e^{-2} + \frac{e^{-2}2^1}{1!} \right]$$
$$= 0.594$$

EXERCISE 3

1   Over a period of time it was shown that a particular daily paper had on average 1.4 misprints per page.

Calculate:

(a) the probability of finding no misprints on a page;

(b) the probability of finding a page with two or more misprints.

2   On average, two per cent of goods on a production line are found to be defective. A random sample of 100 items is taken from production.

(a) What is the mean number of defective goods in a sample of 100?

(b) Use a suitable binomial model to find the probability of:

(i) no defective items in the batch;

(ii) at least one defective item in the batch.

(c) Repeat the calculations in (b) using the Poisson distribution to approximate the binomial probabilities.

3   If $X \sim \mathrm{P}(5)$, calculate

(a) $\mathrm{P}(X = 0)$

(b) $\mathrm{P}(X = 2)$

(c) $\mathrm{P}(X \geqslant 2)$

4   On average, customers arrive at a supermarket check-out till at the rate of 2.4 per minute. A queue begins to develop if more than three people arrive in a given minute. Use a Poisson model to find the probability that a queue develops.

After studying this chapter you should:

1   be familiar with the geometric, binomial and Poisson distributions and the situations they describe;

2   be able to calculate the probabilities of events described by these distributions.

It's a girl

What is the probability of there being eight or more male births before the first female is born?

Let X be the number of births before the first female birth.

In Britain, it is slightly more likely that a baby is a boy. From census data, you can estimate the probability of a girl as 0.487 and a boy as 0.513.

If you count the number of births before a girl, the possible events are G, BG, BBG, BBBG. . . These can be illustrated by a tree diagram.

1   Draw a tree diagram to illustrate the outcomes. What assumptions do you need to make when drawing the tree diagram?

2   Use the tree diagram to write down the probability that the first female birth occurs at:

   (a) the first delivery;

   (b) the second delivery;

   (c) the fifth delivery;

   (d) the nth delivery.

3   Use your answers to question 2 to complete the probability distribution for X, the number of children up to and including the first girl, for values of X up to 7. (Round the probabilities to 3 significant figures.)

4   Calculate the probability of eight or more boys being born before the first girl.

5   For a series of independent trials, let p be the probability that a chosen outcome occurs on any one particular trial. Let X be the number of trials needed to obtain the chosen outcome.

   If $q = 1 - p$, show that:

   (a) $P(X = 1) = p$

   (b) $P(X = 3) = q^2 p$

   (c) $P(X = n) = q^{n-1} p$

Notice that the sequence of probabilities $p, qp, q^2 p, q^3 p, \ldots$ forms a geometric series with common ratio q.

Programming the binomial TASKSHEET 2E

It can be convenient to calculate binomial probabilites by developing a step-by-step or iterative method.

You know:

$$P(X = r) = \binom{n}{r} p^r q^{n-r}$$

and:

$$\binom{n}{r} = \frac{n!}{r!(n-r)!}$$

You need to find a relationship between P($r + 1$) and P(r).

1 Show that:

$$\frac{r!}{(r-1)!} = r$$

2 Find, in terms of r, expressions for:

(a) $\dfrac{(r+1)!}{r!}$

(b) $\dfrac{(r+1)!}{(r-1)!}$

(c) $\dfrac{(r+2)!}{r!}$

(d) $\dfrac{(r+n)!}{r!}$

3 Show that:

$$\frac{\binom{n}{r+1}}{\binom{n}{r}} = \frac{n-r}{r+1}$$

Hence show that:

$$P(r+1) = \left(\frac{n-r}{r+1}\right)\frac{p}{q} P(r)$$

39

The following expression is ideal for programming a computer or calculator.

$$P(r + 1) = \frac{(n - r)}{(r + 1)} \frac{p}{q} P(r)$$

An outline of an algorithm for doing this is as shown.

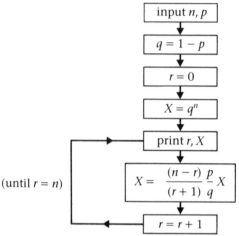

(until $r = n$)

Use this to program your computer or calculator. Check your program by calculating B(10, 0.25), the distribution of which is given in the table.

X	P(X = r)
0	0.0563
1	0.1877
2	0.2816
3	0.2503
4	0.1460
5	0.0584
6	0.0162
7	0.0031
8	0.0003
9	0.0000
10	0.0000

You may choose to retain this program on your calculator for future use.

4 Use the program to calculate the following probability distributions:

(a) B(3, $\frac{1}{4}$)   (b) B(4, $\frac{1}{3}$)

Emergency deliveries

It is possible to find **approximate** binomial models which describe the demands on the emergency system.

On average, requests for deliveries are made four times in a 12-hour period. Assume that in each hour no more than one request can be made. So for each hour:

$$P(\text{request}) \quad = \tfrac{1}{3}$$
$$P(\text{no request}) = \tfrac{2}{3}$$

and the total number of requests in 12 hours will be $B(12, \tfrac{1}{3})$.

1 (a) Show that this model has the correct mean.

 (b) Complete the probability distribution of X:

X	0	1	2	3	4	5	6	7	8	9	10	11	12
$P(X = x)$	?	0.046	0.127	0.212	?	0.191	0.111	0.048	?	0.003	0	0	0

This model is not very realistic since there could be more than one request in any one hour. Suppose you assumed that no more than one request is made in each 15-minute interval.

2 (a) For any 15-minute interval, calculate P(request).

 (b) Define a binomial distribution of X using the assumption that no more than one request is made in each 15-minute interval.

There could still be more than one request made in a 15-minute interval although this is less likely than when intervals of an hour were considered. Suppose you consider one-minute intervals.

3 Given that no more than one request is made in any one minute, find a binomial model for X.

4 Take intervals of 6 seconds ($\tfrac{1}{10}$ minute) and define the binomial distribution for X.

You could continue this process of considering smaller and smaller intervals of time and assuming at most one event in each interval. The smaller the interval you choose, the more realistic will be the binomial model obtained.

This is equivalent to taking a series of binomial distributions B(n, p), where the mean np is constant (equal to 4) but n increases and p decreases. The probabilities associated with each of the distributions you have defined for X are summarised in the table.

X	B($12, \frac{1}{3}$)	B($48, \frac{1}{12}$)	B($720, \frac{1}{180}$)	B($7200, \frac{1}{1800}$)
0	0.008	0.015	0.018	0.018
1	0.046	0.067	0.073	0.073
2	0.127	0.143	0.146	0.147
3	0.212	0.199	0.196	0.195
4	0.238	0.204	0.196	0.195
5	0.191	0.163	0.157	0.156
6	0.111	0.106	0.104	0.104
7	0.048	0.058	0.060	0.060
8	0.015	0.027	0.030	0.030
9	0.003	0.011	0.013	0.013
10	0.000	0.004	0.005	0.005

From the table, you can see that these distributions seem to tend to a limiting distribution, which can be assumed to be the true distribution of X.

5 For each distribution, show that $np = 4$.

The correct probability distribution for X, for which the above binomial models are approximations, is given by the formula:

$$P(X = r) = \frac{e^{-4}4^{r}}{r!}$$

6 What is the significance of the 4 in this expression?

(This result is justified on tasksheet 3E.)

7 Confirm that this formula gives the same probability distribution (to 3 s.f.) as B($7200, \frac{1}{1800}$) above.

8 Calculate the probability of four or more requests using the probability distribution:

$$P(X = r) = \frac{e^{-4}4^{r}}{r!} \qquad \text{where } r = 0, 1, 2, 3, \ldots$$

From binomial to Poisson

You saw in tasksheet 3 that the binomial distribution $B(n, p)$ appears to 'tend to' the Poisson distribution $P(\lambda)$, when:

$$\lambda = np \quad \text{and} \quad n \rightarrow \infty$$

As you are a mathematician you will want to know why!

You showed (on tasksheet 2E) that, for a binomial random variable:

$$P(X = r + 1) = \left(\frac{n - r}{r + 1}\right)\frac{p}{q} P(X = r) \quad \text{and} \quad P(X = 0) = q^n$$

1 For a Poisson random variable, show that:

$$P(X = r + 1) = \frac{\lambda}{r + 1} P(X = r) \quad \text{and} \quad P(X = 0) = e^{-\lambda}.$$

You need to show that as $n \rightarrow \infty$ and $p \rightarrow 0$, with $np = \lambda$:

(A) $q^n \rightarrow e^{-\lambda}$

(B) $\dfrac{n - r}{r + 1}\dfrac{p}{q} \rightarrow \dfrac{\lambda}{r + 1}$

Maclaurin's series for e^x is:

$$e^x = 1 + \frac{x}{1!} + \frac{x^2}{2!} + \frac{x^3}{3!} + \ldots$$

2 Find Maclaurin's series for $e^{-\lambda}$.

3 Show that:

$$q^n = \left(1 - \frac{\lambda}{n}\right)^n$$

Find the first four terms of the binomial expansion.

4 Deduce that as $n \rightarrow \infty$, $q^n \rightarrow e^{-\lambda}$. This demonstrates (A).

5 To demonstrate (B), show that:

$$\frac{(n - r)p}{q} = \frac{\left(1 - \dfrac{r}{n}\right)}{\left(1 - \dfrac{r}{n}\right)}\lambda$$

Deduce that as $n \rightarrow \infty$, $\dfrac{(n - r)p}{q} \rightarrow \lambda$ and hence $\dfrac{(n - r)}{(r + 1)}\dfrac{p}{q} \rightarrow \dfrac{\lambda}{r + 1}$.

4 Selecting and testing the models

4.1 Choosing a suitable model

A basketball player counts the number
of shots he takes to score a basket.
He records the following data:

Shots taken	Frequency
1	10
2	11
3	9
4	8
5	3
6	2
7	0
8	1

(a) Of the models you have considered for counting cases,
which do you think is the most suitable here? Consider
carefully the reasons for your choice.

(b) What assumptions need to be made for your chosen model
to be suitable?

For each variable, suggest whether the binomial, Poisson or
geometric are likely to be suitable models. State assumptions
you need to make and define the model where possible.

(a) The number of sixes obtained when five dice are thrown.

(b) The number of throws needed before you obtain a six on a
die.

(c) The number of boys in families of four children.

(d) The number of clicks made by a geiger counter in a
five-second interval.

(e) The number of home matches a team plays before they
score a goal.

E X E R C I S E   1

1 A survey of 300 families with five children produced the following results for the number of boys (X) in the family.

Number of boys (X)	Number of families
0	7
1	37
2	82
3	104
4	54
5	16
Total	300

(a) Explain why these data might be modelled by a binomial distribution and state the assumptions necessary to use $X \sim B(5, \frac{1}{2})$ as a model.

(b) Use the chi-squared distribution to test $X \sim B(5, \frac{1}{2})$.

(c) Use the data to obtain p, the probability of a male birth and test $X \sim B(5, p)$. Take care over the number of degrees of freedom for the χ^2 test.

(d) Which of the two models best fits this data set? Give a reason for your choice.

2E Four drawing pins are thrown into the air and the number (N) landing point up is counted.

(a) Explain why N has a binomial distribution.

The four pins are thrown 300 times with the following results:

Number landing point up (N)	Frequency
0	10
1	48
2	120
3	86
4	36

(b) (i) Calculate the mean number landing point up and hence obtain an estimate of p, the probability that a pin lands point up.

(ii) Use the χ^2 test to assess the suitability of $N \sim B(4, p)$ as a model for the data.

4.2 The geometric distribution as a model

You may have considered the geometric distribution as a suitable model for the basketball data.

Shots taken	Frequency
1	10
2	11
3	9
4	8
5	3
6	2
7	0
8	1

The geometric distribution, $G(p)$, depends only on the probability p of the event. Since you have no prior information on which to base a value for p, it must be obtained from the data. Remember that this provides a constraint which reduces the number of degrees of freedom by one when you conduct the χ^2 test.

> The data show that the player scored 44 baskets out of 126 shots. How is this worked out?

Set up a model

An estimate of the probability of scoring a basket is:

$$P(\text{scoring a basket}) = \frac{44}{126}$$
$$= 0.349$$

Suppose that $X \sim G(0.349)$ where X is the number of shots needed to score a basket.

The probability distribution and expected frequencies are as follows:

X	$P(X)$	Expected frequency
1	0.349	15.4
2	0.227	10.0
3	0.148	6.5
4	0.096	4.2
5	0.063	2.8
6	0.041	1.8
7	0.027	1.2
$\geqslant 8$	0.049	2.2

Analyse the problem

To apply a chi-squared test, you need to ensure that the cells have **expected frequencies of at least five** to ensure that X^2 has approximately a χ^2 distribution. You can do this by combining the cells as indicated to obtain the following:

X	Observed frequencies	Expected frequencies
1	10	15.4
2	11	10.0
3	9	6.5
4 or 5	11	7.0
6 or more	3	5.2

Show that $X^2 = 6.2$ (to 2 s.f.).

There are five cells, and as p is estimated from the data, there are two constraints.

What are the two constraints?

Testing X^2 with three degrees of freedom, $X^2 > 7.81$ in 5% of samples. Since $6.2 < 7.81$, the proposed model is not rejected at the 5% level.

Interpret /validate

The geometric distribution with $p = 0.349$ is a good model for the data given.

TASKSHEET 1 — Geometric models (page 52)

4.3 Fitting a Poisson distribution to data

In the next tasksheet, you will apply Poisson models to a number of different situations and consider some properties of the distribution.

TASKSHEET 2 — Fitting the Poisson model (page 53)

There are many situations where you can identify an event which is occurring randomly and independently in time (or space), but with a fixed average number of occurrences per unit interval of time (or space).

Randomly occurring event	Unit of time or space
A case of appendicitis is diagnosed	A day in hospital
A geiger counter clicks	A 5-second interval
A telephone rings	A 15-minute interval
A water flea is found	A jar of pond water

Examples of this kind are called **Poisson processes**, and in so far as they fit the conditions above, can be modelled effectively by the Poisson distribution.

One feature of the data which appears to conform to the Poisson model is that the mean for the data appears to be roughly equal in value to the variance. This is confirmed mathematically later, but is a useful rough test to apply to data which you think might be effectively modelled by the Poisson distribution.

> If X is a random variable with a Poisson probability distribution:
>
> $$\text{Mean}(X) = \text{Variance}(X)$$

You can now apply the Poisson probability model to make inferences, as in example 1.

EXAMPLE 1

After a nuclear accident, the number of cases of thyroid disease in babies born in the vicinity was eleven. The average for an equivalent period in the same vicinity was three. Model the situation with a Poisson distribution, stating the assumptions behind the model. Does this provide evidence that the nuclear accident increased the risk of thyroid disease?

SOLUTION

Let X be the number of occurrences of thyroid disease in babies. Then X is a Poisson variable with mean 3, assuming that:

- the same vicinity and length of period are considered;

- thyroid disease occurs randomly in babies;

- incidences of thyroid disease in babies occur independently.

On the basis of the model:

$$P(X \geqslant 11) = 1 - P(X \leqslant 10)$$
$$P(X \leqslant 10) = P(0) + P(1) + \ldots + P(10)$$
$$= e^{-3} + 3e^{-3} + \frac{3^2 e^{-3}}{2!} + \ldots + \frac{3^{10} e^{-3}}{10!}$$
$$= 0.9997$$
$$\Rightarrow P(X \geqslant 11) = 0.0003$$

It is therefore extremely unlikely that this number of cases of thyroid disease in babies would have occurred by chance.

Of course, this in itself does not prove that the nuclear accident caused the increase in thyroid disease in babies – there may have been other factors present. However, it does suggest that a possible connection is worth further investigation.

EXERCISE 2

1   The numbers of people arriving at a post office queue in each of 60 consecutive one-minute intervals are summarised in the table.

Number of arrivals (X)	0	1	2	3	4	5
Number of one minutes (f)	15	19	19	5	1	1

(a) Calculate the mean and variance of the number of people arriving in a one-minute interval.

(b) Explain why the Poisson model might be considered a suitable model for the data.

2 Pityriasis rosea is a skin disorder which has never been shown to be infectious. The number of cases reported in each of 100 consecutive weeks in a particular town was recorded. The data are summarised in the table.

Number of cases (X)	0	1	2	3	4	5	6	7
Number of weeks (f)	31	34	22	8	3	1	0	1

(a) Justify the use of a Poisson model for these data.

(b) Obtain the 'expected' frequencies based on a suitable Poisson probability model.

(c) Conduct a χ^2 goodness of fit test to assess the suitability of the model chosen.

3 A statistician, Ladislaus von Bortkiewicz, published a pamphlet in 1898 which provided one of the most famous examples of data which seem to have a Poisson distribution. The number of men killed by horse kicks each year was recorded for each of the fourteen corps in the Prussian army from 1875 to 1894. The data are summarised below.

Men killed (X)	0	1	2	3	4	5+	Total
Observed frequency	144	91	32	11	2	0	280

(a) Calculate the probabilities with which X takes each of the values shown in the data using the sample mean as an estimate of λ.

(b) Calculate the expected frequencies on the basis of this model.

(c) Compare the observed and expected frequencies and comment on whether you think the Poisson distribution you have used is a good fit for the data.

(d) Conduct a χ^2 goodness of fit test on the model and comment on your findings.

After studying this chapter you should:

1   be able to choose a suitable probability model for counting cases data;

2   be able to set up and test a chosen model;

3   know how to calculate the number of degrees of freedom when modelling with the binomial, geometric and Poisson distributions;

4   know that the mean and variance for data having a Poisson distribution are approximately equal;

5   be able to make simple inferences on the basis of a chosen model.

Geometric models

You will need a calculator or tables for obtaining random numbers.

It will be better to work in pairs or small groups to collect the relevant data.

Random digits (0, 1, 2, . . ., 9) are produced so that each has an equal probability of occurrence. Count the number of digits that occur up to the occurrence of the first zero. This is called the **run length**.

1, 3, 9, 7, 0	five digits needed
3, 6, 0	three digits needed
0	one digit needed

1 Use your random number generator and count the digits generated up to and including the first zero. Repeat about 200 times and complete the table.

Length of run (L)	1	2	3	4	. . .
Number of runs					

2 State the assumptions necessary to use $L \sim G(\frac{1}{10})$ as a model here. Why does $p = \frac{1}{10}$?

3 Set up and test the $G(\frac{1}{10})$ model against your data. Take care to combine groups as necessary when using the χ^2 test. This, of course, has an effect on the number of degrees of freedom for the test.

4 Use the data to calculate p, where p is the probability of obtaining a run of length one.

5 Set up and test an alternative model $G(p)$. Which of the two models is the best for your data? Why?

6 Calculate the mean run length for your data.

Fitting the Poisson model

You will need:
- A computer
- A stop-watch
- The program *Stars*
  or
- The program *Bleeps*

To fit a Poisson distribution, the only 'parameter' you need to know is the mean, μ. This is usually estimated from the data and, when applying a chi-squared goodness of fit test, adds a constraint to the observed frequencies and so reduces the number of degrees of freedom by one. You also need to combine cells in which the expected frequency falls below 5.

You should do either experiment A or experiment B.

A   Run the program *Stars*, which simulates a random pattern of 'stars' on the computer screen. A 7×7 grid is superimposed on the 'star map'. Record the frequency distribution of number of stars per grid square. (You will need to decide how to deal with stars lying on the lines.) Illustrate this distribution with a bar chart. Calculate the mean number of stars per square, and the variance of this number. Use the sample mean to fit a Poisson distribution to the data you have collected. Test for goodness of fit.

B   Run the program *Bleeps*. This bleeps at random times, with an average number of bleeps, μ, per 10-second interval, where μ is input. Calculate the sample mean and variance and illustrate the data with a bar chart. Fit a Poisson distribution to the data and test for goodness of fit.

1   The following data refer to the numbers of water fleas present in 50 samples of pond water.

Number of water fleas	2	3	4	5	6	7	8	9	10	11	12	13	14	15	16
Number of samples	1	1	2	2	2	6	7	4	5	7	3	5	3	1	1

Find the mean and variance of the data.

2   Represent the data with a bar chart.

3   Fit a Poisson distribution to the data and test using the chi-squared distribution.

5 Forming new variables

5.1 Games of chance

So far, the situations you have studied have each involved a single variable together with its associated probability distribution. There are many interesting situations where **combining** random variables arises in some way. The chapter begins by considering **discrete random variables** and later extends the results to **continuous variables**.

As an illustration, consider a game which has two options.

Option 1: Two dice are thrown and you win 1p for each point. Your score is the **total** score showing on the two dice.

Option 2: A single die is thrown and you win 1p per point, your score being double that shown on the die.

> The entry price is the same for both games. Which would you choose to play and why?

TASKSHEET 1 — Combining variables (page 65)

You have considered combining random variables in two ways:

- adding two (or more) together, for example, $R + B, R + R$, etc.;
- multiplying by a constant, for example, $2R, 5B$, etc.

The experience gained from tasksheet 1 should lead you to conjecture that:

> Mean $(X + Y)$ = mean (X) + mean (Y)
> Variance $(X + Y)$ = variance (X) + variance (Y)
>
> Mean $(aX) = a \times$ mean (X)
> Variance $(aX) = a^2 \times$ variance (X)

You should note that the variables you have combined have been **independent** and **discrete**. The results obtained above can be proved for all independent random variables.

E X A M P L E   1

Two people play a game in which each has a spinner. The score is counted as the total of the score on each spinner. The probability distributions for the two spinners are:

Spinner 1			
Score	1	2	3
Probability	$\frac{1}{2}$	$\frac{1}{4}$	$\frac{1}{4}$

Spinner 2		
Score	2	4
Probability	$\frac{1}{4}$	$\frac{3}{4}$

It costs 20p to have a go and you win five times the total score on the two spinners in pence.

(a) Calculate the probability of a score of five.

(b) What is the most likely score?

(c) Calculate your expected winnings per turn.

S O L U T I O N

(a) $P(\text{total} = 5) = P(1, 4) + P(3, 2)$
$$= \tfrac{1}{2} \times \tfrac{3}{4} + \tfrac{1}{4} \times \tfrac{1}{4} \qquad \text{(the events are independent)}$$
$$= \tfrac{7}{16}$$

(b) The most likely score is a five. The most likely outcome is a one on spinner 1 with a four on spinner 2.
$$P(1, 4) = \tfrac{1}{2} \times \tfrac{3}{4} = \tfrac{3}{8}$$

(c) Expected winnings $= (5 \times \text{mean score}) - 20$
Expected score $= \text{mean}(S_1 + S_2)$
$= \text{mean}(S_1) + \text{mean}(S_2)$

$\text{Mean}(S_1) = \tfrac{7}{4}, \quad \text{mean}(S_2) = \tfrac{14}{4}$
$\Rightarrow \text{Mean}(S_1 + S_2) = \tfrac{7}{4} + \tfrac{14}{4} = \tfrac{21}{4}$

The winnings are $\dfrac{5 \times 21}{4} - 20 = 6.25\text{p}$

You would expect to win an average of 6.25 pence per game.

Use these ideas and results to analyse the dice game described at the beginning of this chapter.

EXERCISE 1

1   A board game uses a cuboid roller with square cross-section to determine
    how many places forward a player moves. The four rectangular faces are
    numbered 1, 2, 5 and 8.

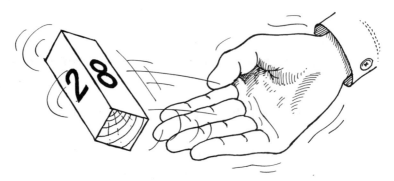

(a) If X is the score obtained by rolling the cuboid, find:

(i) mean (X) (ii) variance (X)

(b) If, during the game, a player lands on a yellow square, the next score on
    the roller is doubled. Find the mean and variance of the doubled scores.

(c) If, during the game, a player lands on a red square, the next score on the
    roller is trebled. Find the mean and variance of the trebled scores.

(d) Write down the mean and variance of the total score obtained when
    two identical rollers are used together.

2   (a) An ordinary die has its faces numbered 1, 2, 2, 3, 3 and 4. If X is the score
        obtained by rolling the die, find the mean and variance of the scores.

(b) A second die has its faces numbered 2, 4, 4, 6, 6 and 8. What are the
    mean and variance of the scores?

(c) Write down the mean and variance of the total score when both dice are
    rolled.

5.2 Combining by subtraction

(a) Using the program *DComb*, investigate combinations of variables such as $(R - Y)$, $(B - Y)$, etc. Conjecture a result for the mean and variance of $(X - Y)$ in relation to the mean and variance of X and Y.

(b) List the probability distribution for $(A - B)$ where A and B have probability distributions as follows:

A	0	1	2
$P(A)$	0.2	0.6	0.2

B	1	2
$P(B)$	0.5	0.5

(c) Confirm that

  (i) mean$(A - B)$ = mean(A) − mean(B);

  (ii) variance$(A - B)$ = variance(A) + variance(B).

The earlier results on combining random variables can be simply extended.

> For **independent** random variables, X and Y:
>
> $$\text{mean } (X \pm Y) = \text{mean}(X) \pm \text{mean}(Y)$$
>
> $$\text{variance } (X \pm Y) = \text{variance}(X) + \text{variance}(Y)$$

EXAMPLE 2

Independent random variables A, B and C have the following means and variances:

	A	B	C
Mean	4	2	3
Variance	2	1	2

Write down the mean and variance of:

(a) $2A - B$

(b) $A + B - C$

(c) $2A + 2B - 3C$

SOLUTION

(a) Mean $(2A - B) = 2\,\text{mean}(A) - \text{mean}(B)$
$$= 6$$
Variance$(2A - B) = 2^2\,\text{variance}(A) + \text{variance}(B)$
$$= 9$$

(b) Mean$(A + B - C)$ $\qquad = 4 + 2 - 3$
$\qquad\qquad\qquad\qquad\qquad = 3$
Variance$(A + B - C)$ $\quad = 2 + 1 + 2$
$\qquad\qquad\qquad\qquad\qquad = 5$

(c) Mean$(2A + 2B - 3C)$ $\quad = 2 \times 4 + 2 \times 2 - 3 \times 3$
$\qquad\qquad\qquad\qquad\qquad = 3$
Variance$(2A + 2B - 3C) = 2^2 \times 2 + 2^2 \times 1 + 3^2 \times 2$
$\qquad\qquad\qquad\qquad\qquad = 30$

5.3 Combining Poisson variables

For Poisson variables, the following result can be proved.

> If X and Y are independently distributed Poisson variables having means λ and γ respectively, then $X + Y$ is also a Poisson variable:
>
> $$X + Y \sim P(\lambda + \gamma)$$

EXAMPLE 3

Cars stopping at a roadside garage come from either the north-bound or south-bound traffic. On average, there are three cars from the south-bound lane in a 15-minute interval and 1.6 cars from the north-bound lane every 15 minutes. The number of arrivals has a Poisson distribution in both cases.

Calculate the probability that there are:

(a) no cars from the north in a 15-minute interval;

(b) more than two cars in a 15-minute interval.

SOLUTION

(a) Let the number of cars stopping from the north be N.
$N \sim P(1.6)$
$P(N = 0) = e^{-1.6} = 0.202$

(b) The total number of cars stopping is $T = N + S$
$T \sim P(3 + 1.6)$
$T \sim P(4.6)$
$P(T > 2) = 1 - P(T = 0, 1, 2)$

$$= 1 - \left(e^{-4.6} + 4.6e^{-4.6} + \frac{4.6^2 e^{-4.6}}{2!} \right)$$

$$= 1 - e^{-4.6} \left(1 + 4.6 + \frac{4.6^2}{2} \right)$$

$$= 0.837$$

EXERCISE 2

1 A and B are random variables having means μ_A and μ_B and variances σ_A^2 and σ_B^2 respectively.

Write down the mean and variance of the variables:

(a) $A + B$

(b) $2A$

(c) $3A - B$

2 X and Y have independent Poisson distributions, where:

$$X \sim P(4) \quad \text{and} \quad Y \sim P(3)$$

(a) Write down the mean of $X + Y$.

(b) Calculate the probability that $X + Y < 4$.

3   An executive has two telephones on her desk which receive calls independently. The number of calls received by each telephone has a Poisson distribution with, on average, three calls per 5-minute interval on one and two calls per 5-minute interval on the other.

(a) Write down the mean and variance of the **total** number of calls received in a 5-minute interval.

(b) If the distribution of the total number of calls is also Poisson, find the probability that the number of calls received in any 5-minute interval is:

(i) zero,

(ii) more than two.

5.4 Expectation

There is a convenient notation for the **expected value** of a random variable.

> The **expected value**, or **expectation**, of a random variable (X) is the mean value of the variable. It is written E[X].

$$\text{Mean}(X) \;=\; \sum_i x_i P(x_i)$$
$$= E[X]$$
$$\text{Mean}(2X) \;=\; \sum_i 2x_i P(x_i)$$
$$= E[2X]$$
$$\text{Mean}(X^2) \;=\; \sum_i x_i^2 P(x_i)$$
$$= E[X^2]$$

One of the results obtained earlier can therefore be written:

$$E[X + Y] = E[X] + E[Y]$$

EXAMPLE 4

The probability distribution of X is given below. Find the expected value of X^3.

x	1	2
P($X = x$)	0.2	0.8

SOLUTION

X^3 can take the values 1^3 and 2^3 with probabilities 0.2 and 0.8 respectively.

$$E[X^3] = 1^3 \times 0.2 + 2^3 \times 0.8$$
$$= 6.6$$

Find E[$2X^2$].

A convenient shorthand for the variance is $V(X)$. The variance may be defined in terms of expectations as follows:

$$V[X] = \sum_i x_i^2 P(x_i) - (\bar{x})^2$$

But $\sum_i x_i^2 P(x_i) = E[X^2]$

and $\qquad \bar{x} = E[X]$

So:

$$V[X] = E[X^2] - (E[X])^2$$

Show that:

(a) $E[aX] = aE[X]$

(b) $V[aX] = a^2 V[X]$

The results of section 5.2 may be written using this new notation as follows:

$$E[X \pm Y] = E[X] \pm E[Y]$$
$$V[X \pm Y] = V[X] + V[Y]$$
$$E[aX] = a \times E[X]$$
$$V[aX] = a^2 \times V[X]$$

EXAMPLE 5

Two random variables X and Y are such that $E(X) = V(X) = 1$, $E(Y) = 3$ and $V(Y) = 2$.
Find:

(a) $E(X - Y)$

(b) $V(3X - 2Y)$

SOLUTION

(a) $E(X - Y) = E(X) - E(Y) = -2$

(b) $V(3X - 2Y) = V(3X) + V(2Y)$
$$= 3^2 V(X) + 2^2 V(Y)$$
$$= 17$$

5.5 The mean and variance of B(n, p) – a proof

The results of the previous sections can be used to prove results for the mean and variance of a binomial random variable. A binomial variable occurs when you are considering the total number of times a given event occurs in n independent trials. For example, the trial might be the throwing of a coin and the outcome might be the occurrence of a head. The total number of heads occurring when, for example, four coins are thrown would be a binomial random variable taking values of 0, 1, 2, 3 or 4.

Suppose the outcome of a particular trial occurs with probability p and does not occur with probability $(1 - p)$ or q.

There are 0 or 1 occurrences in a given trial.

Let X be the number of occurrences in a trial.

$X = \{0, 1\}$

The probability distribution for X is:

x	0	1
$P(X = x)$	q	p

Show that the mean and variance of X are p and pq respectively.

Now, for n trials, define the binomial variable R, where:

$$R = X_1 + X_2 + \ldots + X_n \quad \text{and} \quad R \sim B(n, p)$$
$$\Rightarrow E[R] = E[X_1 + X_2 + \ldots + X_n]$$
$$= E[X_1] + E[X_2] + \ldots + E[X_n] \quad ①$$
$$= E[X] + E[X] + \ldots + E[X] \quad ②$$
$$= n \times E[X]$$
$$= np$$

In the argument given above, explain why lines ① and ② are correct.

63

Also, for the variance $V[R]$,

$$V[R] = V[X_1 + X_2 + \ldots + X_n]$$
$$= V[X_1] + V[X_2] + \ldots + V[X_n]$$
$$= V[X] + V[X] + \ldots + V[X]$$
$$= nV[X]$$
$$= npq$$

If $R \sim B(n, p)$ then:

$$E[R] = np$$
$$V[R] = npq$$

TASKSHEET 2E – *Some proofs (page 67)*

After working through this chapter you should:

1 know that random variables may be combined to give composite variables;

2 understand the term expectation as applied to random variables and be familiar with the notation of expectation;

3 know that for **independent** random variables:

(a) $E(X \pm Y) = E(X) \pm E(Y)$

(b) $V(X \pm Y) = V(X) + V(Y)$

4 be able to obtain the formulas for the mean and variance of a binomial random variable.

Combining variables

You will need:

- The program *DComb*
- Chance cards

Recall the yellow chance cards. The probability distribution of Y, the score on a card, is as shown in the table.

y	1	2	3	4	Mean = 2
$P(Y = y)$	0.4	0.3	0.2	0.1	Variance = 1

For the blue pack, the distribution is:

b	1	2	3	Mean = 2
$P(B = b)$	0.25	0.50	0.25	Variance = 0.5

1 A game consists of selecting a card at random from the yellow pack and noting its score (Y). It is replaced and the pack shuffled. A second card is then selected from the blue pack (B) and the total score ($Y + B$) recorded.

Complete the table, which shows all possible totals ($Y + B$).

		Score on blue card		
		1	2	3
Score on	1	2	3	
yellow card	2			
	3			
	4			7

The probability of obtaining a score of 3 is:
$$P(3) = P(1, 2) + P(2, 1)$$
$$= P(1)P(2) + P(2)P(1)$$
$$= 0.4 \times 0.5 + 0.3 \times 0.25$$
$$= 0.275$$

2 (a) Show that $P(5) = 0.20$ and complete the probability distribution for the total
score $Y + B$.

Score $Y + B$	Probability
2	
3	0.275
4	
5	0.20
6	0.10
7	

(b) Find the mean and variance of $Y + B$.
How are the mean and variance of $Y + B$ related to those of Y and B?

For the remainder of this tasksheet you should work with the program *DComb*, which
allows you to choose cards from the yellow, red or blue packs. You might, for example,
decide to have a game where the score is found by adding the scores on a red (R) and a
blue (B) card. This would be $R + B$. *DComb* will calculate the mean and variance for each
game chosen, simulating a large number of selections of cards.

3 (a) Using *DComb*, obtain the mean and variance for the following games:

   (i) $R + B$ (ii) $R + B + Y$

   (iii) $Y + R$ (iv) $R + R$

(b) Use your results to conjecture a result showing how the mean and variance of
$X + Y$ are related to those of X and Y.

4 Use *DComb* to enable you to conjecture a result linking the mean and variance of
(aX) to that of X where a is a constant.

5 Predict results for the mean and variance of:

(a) $2R + Y$

(b) $3R + 2Y$

(c) $2R + 3B + Y$

Some proofs

Of the three discrete distributions considered in chapter 3 – geometric, binomial and Poisson – a proof of the results for the mean and variance has, so far, only been given for the binomial. On this tasksheet, you will consider the other two distributions.

The geometric distribution

If $X \sim G(p)$, then $E(X)$ is the number of trials needed before the required event occurs.

> **1** How long do you think you would wait, on average, before scoring a six when you throw a die?

If $X \to G(p)$ then $E[X] = \sum_i x_i P(x_i)$

Writing this out in full gives:

$$E[X] = 1p + 2pq + 3pq^2 + \ldots$$
$$= p(1 + 2q + 3q^2 + \ldots)$$

> **2** **Confirm** that the expression in brackets is the binomial expansion of $(1 - q)^{-2}$.

$$E[X] = \frac{p}{(1 - q)^2} = \frac{1}{p}$$

For throwing a six with a die, $X \sim G(\frac{1}{6})$. You would expect to wait six throws on average because $E(X) = 6$.

The Poisson distribution

Suppose X is a Poisson variable, $X \sim P(\lambda)$.
The following series for e^x will prove useful.

$$e^x = 1 + x + \frac{x^2}{2!} + \frac{x^3}{2!} + \ldots + \frac{x^n}{n!} + \ldots$$

$$E[X] = \sum_i x_i P(x_i) \qquad \text{where } P(X = r) = \frac{e^{-\lambda} \lambda^r}{r!}$$

Complete the following proof.

$$
\begin{aligned}
E[X] &= \frac{0 \times e^{-\lambda} \lambda^0}{0!} + \frac{1 \times e^{-\lambda} \lambda}{1!} + \ldots \\
&= e^{-\lambda}\{(\ldots) + (\ldots) + (\ldots) + \ldots\} \\
&= \lambda e^{-\lambda}\{\ldots + \ldots + \ldots + \ldots\} \\
&= \lambda e^{-\lambda} e^{\lambda} \qquad \text{using the expansion of } e^x \\
&= \lambda
\end{aligned}
$$

To obtain the variance, use:

$$V[X] = E[X^2] - (E[X])^2 \qquad \text{where } E[X] = \lambda$$

Finding $E[X^2]$ is awkward here. It is best to use an algebraic 'trick' and to work with $E[X(X - 1)]$.

---

3 Show that:

$$E[X^2] = E[X(X - 1)] + E[X]$$

First find $E[X(X - 1)]$.

$$
\begin{aligned}
E[X(X - 1)] &= \sum_i x_i(x_i - 1)P(x_i) \\
&= \frac{2 \times 1 \times e^{-\lambda} \lambda^2}{2!} + \frac{3 \times 2 \times e^{-\lambda} \lambda^3}{3!} + \ldots
\end{aligned}
$$

---

4 Complete the proof, showing:

(a) $E[X(X - 1)] = \lambda^2$

and hence:

(b) $V[X] = \lambda$

This confirms the result stated for Poisson variables, i.e. that the mean and the variance are equal.

6 Continuous random variables

6.1 The Normal probability density function

This unit has concentrated on **discrete** random variables and some of the important probability models associated with them. There are, of course, models for **continuous** random variables, the single most important being the Normal probability model which you considered earlier in *The Normal distribution*. It would be worth looking at an example as a reminder before considering other continuous probability distributions.

> A machine is set to deliver sugar into bags. The weight of sugar it delivers is Normally distributed, having a mean of 1.1 kg and standard deviation 0.1 kg.
>
> (a) **Approximately** what proportion of bags marked 1 kg will be underweight?
>
> (b) Confirm your answer to (a) by calculating this proportion using Normal tables.

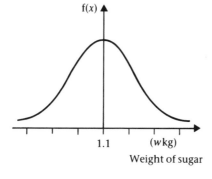

The graph of this distribution is called the **Normal probability density function**.

If X is a continuous random variable, the probability that X takes a value between a and b is given by the area under the probability density function for X, between $X = a$ and $X = b$. In the case of simple functions, this is usually calculated by direct integration or by using tables which give the area in the two important cases of the Normal distribution and the chi-squared distribution.

EXAMPLE 1

A certain manufacturer claims that there are 64 g of real fruit in every 100 g of their jam. The actual weight of fruit in the jam is distributed Normally, having a mean weight of 68 g and standard deviation 1.6 g. Calculate the proportion of 100 g measures of jam which contain:

(a) more than 70 g of fruit;

(b) less than 64 g of fruit.

SOLUTION

Let the weight of fruit in 100 g of jam be W g.
Then $W \sim N(68, 1.6^2)$

(a)

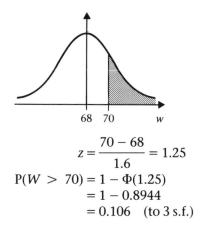

$$z = \frac{70 - 68}{1.6} = 1.25$$

$$\begin{aligned} P(W > 70) &= 1 - \Phi(1.25) \\ &= 1 - 0.8944 \\ &= 0.106 \quad \text{(to 3 s.f.)} \end{aligned}$$

So 10.6% of the 100 g measures will contain more than 70 g of fruit.

(b)

$$z = \frac{64 - 68}{1.6} = -2.5$$

$$\begin{aligned} P(W < 64) &= \Phi(-2.5) \\ &= 1 - \Phi(2.5) \\ &= 0.006 \end{aligned}$$

0.6% of the 100 g measures will contain less than 64 g of fruit.

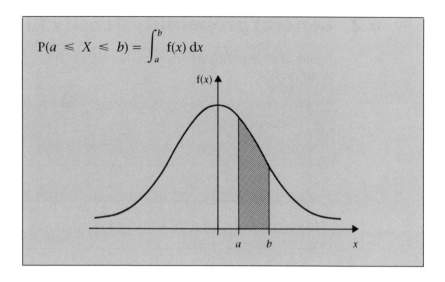

$$P(a \leqslant X \leqslant b) = \int_a^b f(x)\,dx$$

EXERCISE 1

1 My journey to work takes 20 minutes on average, with a standard deviation of 5 minutes. The journey time may be considered to be Normally distributed. If I take longer than 26 minutes, I am late. Calculate the probability of my being late.

2 The length of time that a particular make of light bulb lasts is distributed Normally, having mean 2000 hours and standard deviation 50 hours. Calculate the probability that a particular light bulb will last:

(a) longer than 1970 hours;

(b) between 2050 and 2080 hours.

3 The mean survival period for daisies after being sprayed with a weed killer is 20 days. The survival time is Normally distributed. If a quarter of the daisies are still surving after 23 days, calculate an estimate for the standard deviation of the survival time.

6.2 General probability density functions

A general probability density function $f(x)$ must have the following properties:

- $f(x) \geq 0$ for all x
- The total area under the curve $f(x)$ must be 1.

Explain why $f(x)$ must have these properties.

EXAMPLE 2

A probability density function $f(x)$ is defined as follows.

$$f(x) = \begin{cases} \dfrac{k}{x^2} & \text{for } 1 \leq x \leq 6 \\ 0 & \text{for all other } x \end{cases}$$

Find the value of k.

SOLUTION

$$\int_1^6 f(x)\,dx = 1, \quad \text{so} \quad \int_1^6 \frac{k}{x^2}\,dx = 1$$

$$\Rightarrow k \int_1^6 \frac{1}{x^2}\,dx = 1$$

$$\Rightarrow k \left[-\frac{1}{x} \right]_1^6 = 1$$

$$\Rightarrow k \left[\left(-\frac{1}{6} \right) - \left(-\frac{1}{1} \right) \right] = 1$$

$$\Rightarrow \qquad\qquad \frac{5}{6}k = 1$$

$$\Rightarrow \qquad\qquad k = \frac{6}{5} = 1.2$$

EXAMPLE 3

The incubation period, X days, for a particular infection, is modelled by the probability density function f(x), where f(x) is defined as follows.

$$f(x) = \tfrac{1}{144}(36 - x^2) \qquad \text{for } 0 \leqslant x \leqslant 6$$

What is the probability that you will catch the infection during the second day?

SOLUTION

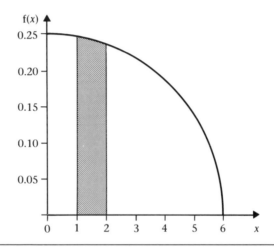

Write down:

 (a) $P(X \geqslant 6)$ (b) $P(X \leqslant 0)$

$$P(1 \leqslant X \leqslant 2) = \int_1^2 f(x)\, dx$$

$$= \int_1^2 \tfrac{1}{144}(36 - x^2)\, dx$$

$$= \tfrac{1}{144}\left[36x - \tfrac{1}{3}x^3 \right]_1^2$$

$$= \tfrac{1}{144}\left[\left(72 - \tfrac{8}{3}\right) - \left(36 - \tfrac{1}{3}\right) \right]$$

$$= 0.23 \qquad \text{(to 2 s.f.)}$$

The probability that you will become infected on the second day is 0.23.

What is the probability of becoming infected on the first day?

EXERCISE 2

In each of the examples, f(x) refers to a probability density function.

1

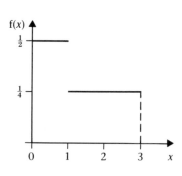

(a) Define the possible values of X.

(b) Show that the area under the graph of f(x) = 1.

(c) Find

    (i) $P(X \geqslant 1)$

    (ii) $P(X \geqslant \frac{1}{2})$

    (iii) $P(\frac{1}{2} \leqslant X \leqslant 2)$

    (iv) $P(X \leqslant 3)$

2 (a) Find k.

    (b) Find:

        (i) $P(X \geqslant 1.5)$

        (ii) $P(X \leqslant 0.5)$

        (iii) $P(0.5 \leqslant X \leqslant 1.5)$

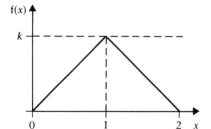

3 In a game, a wooden block is propelled with a stick across a flat deck. On each attempt, the distance, X metres, reached by the block lies between 0 and 10 metres and the variation is measured by the probability density function:

$$f(x) = 0.0012x^2(10 - x)$$

Calculate the probability that the block:

(a) travels more than 5 metres;

(b) travels between 1 and 2 metres.

6.3 The mean and variance

For a discrete variable X, the mean μ was defined by:

$$\mu = \sum_i x_i P(x_i)$$

The analogous form of this definition for a continuous variable X having density function $f(x)$ is:

$$\mu = \int x f(x)\, dx \qquad \text{where the integral is taken over the whole range of } X \text{ values.}$$

For the variance, the expression equivalent to:

$$\sigma^2 = \sum_i x_i^2 P(x_i) - \mu^2 \qquad \text{(for a discrete variable)}$$

is:

$$\sigma^2 = \int x^2 f(x)\, dx - \mu^2 \qquad \text{(for a continuous variable)}$$

If X is a continuous random variable having a probability function $f(X)$ when $a \leqslant X \leqslant b$:

$$\mu = \int_a^b x f(x)\, dx$$

$$\sigma^2 = \int_a^b x^2 f(x)\, dx - \mu^2$$

EXAMPLE 4

X is a continuous random variable and $0 \leqslant x \leqslant 1$. The probability density function of X is $f(x) = 3x^2$. Calculate the mean and variance of X.

SOLUTION

$$\mu = 3 \int_0^1 x f(x)\, dx$$

$$= 3 \int_0^1 x^3\, dx$$

$$= 3 \left[\tfrac{1}{4}x^4 \right]_0^1$$

$$= \tfrac{3}{4}$$

$$\sigma^2 = \int_0^1 x^2 f(x)\, dx - \mu^2$$

$$= 3 \int_0^1 x^4\, dx - (\tfrac{3}{4})^2$$

$$= 3 \left[\tfrac{1}{5}x^5 \right]_0^1 - \tfrac{9}{16}$$

$$= \tfrac{39}{80}$$

EXERCISE 3

1 A random variable X has probability density function $f(x)$, where

$$f(x) = \begin{cases} kx^2 & 0 \leqslant x \leqslant 1 \\ 0 & \text{otherwise} \end{cases}$$

(a) Show that $k = 3$.

(b) Calculate the mean and variance of X.

(c) Find the probability that $X \geqslant 0.5$.

2 A department store will deliver parcels within a range of 5 and 15 miles. The probability of a delivery being for a distance X miles is given by the probability density function $f(x)$, where:

$$f(x) = \begin{cases} \dfrac{k}{x^3} & 5 \leqslant X \leqslant 15 \\ 0 & \text{otherwise} \end{cases}$$

(a) Calculate k and sketch a graph of $f(x)$.

(b) Find the mean delivery distance.

(c) Half of all deliveries are for distances of m miles or more. Find m.

3 The distance (X metres) travelled by a wooden block in a game is given by the probability density function $f(x)$, where:

$$f(x) = \begin{cases} 0.0012x^2(10 - x) & 0 \leqslant x \leqslant 10 \\ 0 & \text{otherwise} \end{cases}$$

Calculate the mean distance travelled.

6.4 The uniform distribution

Motorway signposts give distances to the nearest mile. This means that in any stated distance, the error (X) is between -0.5 and $+0.5$ mile.

> (a) If the distance from Penrith to Appleby is given as 13 miles, then what is the probability that the actual distance is:
>
>   (i) between 13 and 13.5 miles;
>
>   (ii) between 13.25 and 13.5 miles?
>
> (b) Describe the probability distribution of X.

A variable X, which can take values between a and b and for which values in this interval are all equally likely to occur, is said to have a **uniform** distribution.

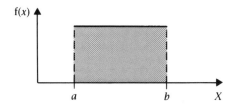

The area of the rectangle must equal 1 because X **must** take a value between a and b. That is:

$$P(a \leqslant X \leqslant b) = 1$$

> Explain why the height of the rectangle is $\dfrac{1}{b-a}$.

The uniform distribution of X is defined as:

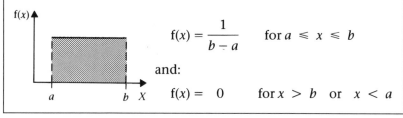

$$f(x) = \frac{1}{b-a} \quad \text{for } a \leqslant x \leqslant b$$

and:

$$f(x) = 0 \quad \text{for } x > b \text{ or } x < a$$

> A random variable, X, is distributed uniformly and can take any value between 2 and 4.
>
> Find the mean and variance of X.

6.5 **The exponential distribution**

You saw earlier that the Poisson distribution described a discrete variable occurring randomly in time or space. For example, if a computer is programmed to 'bleep' on average once every ten seconds, then bleeps might occur as indicated by the arrows.

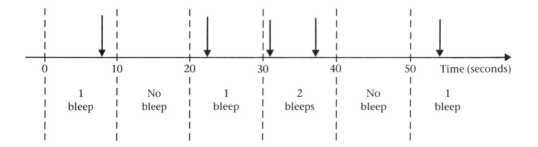

| | 1 bleep | | No bleep | | 1 bleep | | 2 bleeps | | No bleep | | 1 bleep |

It is interesting to consider how long, on average, you would have to wait for a bleep to occur.

A computer bleeps at random once in a second. Having bleeped, how long on average do you expect to wait before the next bleep? Sketch what you think the distribution of T, the length of wait, might look like.

(The program *Bleep 2* will help.)

The distribution which describes the length of wait between random events is known as the **exponential** (or **negative exponential**) **distribution**.

> If X has an exponential distribution, then its probability density function f(x) is:
>
> $$f(x) = \lambda e^{-\lambda x} \qquad \text{for } x \geqslant 0$$

The distribution is determined by fixing the value of λ. Although it will not be proved here, λ is in fact the mean value of X.

Sketch f(x) with $\lambda = 2$.

Explain why the probability density is greatest for small values of x.

EXERCISE 4

1 A computer bleeps randomly, on average once every second. The probability density function describing the time, T, between bleeps is $f(t) = e^{-t}$.

(a) Sketch f(t).

(b) Shade the areas representing the probability of:

   (i) a bleep in the first second;

   (ii) waiting longer than two seconds for a bleep.

(c) Calculate the probability of each event in (b).

2 People join a particular queue at random. The average time between arrivals is two minutes. The time between arrivals (T minutes) has probability density function $f(t) = 2e^{-2t}$. Calculate the probability that:

(a) one person arrives in the first minute;

(b) the next person arrives between one and two minutes later.

6.6 **Combining Normal random variables**

Chapter 4 considered the possibility of combining discrete variables. You can combine continuous random variables in the same way and, indeed, some most important practical applications arise where Normal variables are combined. Remember that the variables being combined must be **independent** of each other.

A common example is illustrated. All passenger lifts have a notice specifying the maximum load and usually state the maximum number of persons that can be carried safely. The maximum number of persons is determined from the maximum load by considering the distribution of the total weight of n adult males. The weight of an adult male is a Normal variable, so the manufacturer needs to consider the problem of adding together Normal variables.

When you add independently distributed Normal variables, you need to know the answers to three questions.

(a) How is the sum **distributed**? Is it also a Normal variable?

(b) What is its mean value and how is this related to the original variables?

(c) What is its variance and how is this related to the original variables?

Questions (b) and (c) were answered in chapter 4. The results you found there also apply to **continuous** variables.

> If $X \sim N(\mu_x, \sigma_x^2)$ and $Y \sim N(\mu_y, \sigma_y^2)$
>
> then:
>
> $$E[X \pm Y] = \mu_x \pm \mu_y$$
> $$V[X \pm Y] = \sigma_x^2 + \sigma_y^2 \,.$$

TASKSHEET 1 — Combining Normal variables (page 85)

Your results may be summarised as follows:

A sum or difference of **independent** Normal random variables is also Normally distributed.

If X and Y are independent random variables, where:

$$X \sim N(\mu_x, \sigma_x^2) \quad \text{and} \quad Y \sim N(\mu_y, \sigma_y^2)$$

then:

$$X + Y \sim N(\mu_x + \mu_y, \sigma_x^2 + \sigma_y^2)$$

and:

$$X - Y \sim N(\mu_x - \mu_y, \sigma_x^2 + \sigma_y^2)$$

These results can be used to solve problems like that of the maximum load for a lift. Some simple examples are given.

EXAMPLE 5

If $X \sim N(10, 2)$ and $Y \sim N(8, 1)$ find $P(X + Y > 20)$

SOLUTION

Variances are added

$X + Y \sim N(10 + 8, 2 + 1)$
$X + Y \sim N(18, 3)$

Standardising the value $X + Y = 20$

$$\Rightarrow z = \frac{20 - 18}{\sqrt{3}}$$

$$= 1.15$$

$$\Rightarrow P(X + Y > 20) = 1 - \Phi(1.15)$$
$$= 1 - 0.875$$
$$= 0.125$$

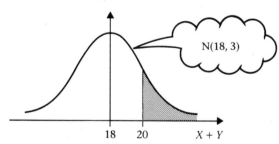

N(18, 3)

18   20 $X + Y$

So, in $12\frac{1}{2}$% of cases the value of the sum of the two variables will be greater than 20.

EXAMPLE 6

The length (in centimetres) of a matchbox is a random variable $X \sim N(5, 0.01)$. The length (in centimetres) of matches to go in the box is a random variable, $Y \sim N(4.6, 0.01)$.

What percentage of matches will not fit in the box?

SOLUTION

The matches will not fit if $Y > X$. This condition can be rearranged as $X - Y < 0$.

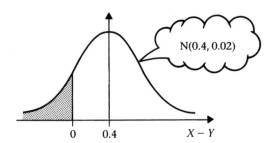

$$E[X - Y] = 5 - 4.6$$
$$= 0.4$$
$$V[X - Y] = 0.01 + 0.01$$
$$= 0.02$$
$$\Rightarrow X - Y \sim N(0.4, 0.02)$$

Add variances

N(0.4, 0.02)

0   0.4 $X - Y$

You need to find the shaded area. Standardising in the usual way:

$$z = \frac{0.0 - 0.4}{\sqrt{(0.02)}}$$
$$= -2.83$$
$$P(Z < 0) = \Phi(-2.83)$$
$$= 1 - \Phi(2.83)$$
$$= 0.0023$$

So only about 0.2% of matches will not fit into the box.

EXERCISE 5

1 A manufacturer of toiletries is producing a special offer pack containing a deodorant spray and a bar of soap. The deodorant spray can has a length (in centimetres) given by the random variable $X \sim N(14, 0.02)$. The soap has a length (in centimetres) given by the random variable $Y \sim N(9, 0.01)$.

Find the probability that the deodorant and soap will not fit a container of length 23.4 cm if they are packed end to end.

2 A bottle of fruit juice has a screw cap which has length (in centimetres) given by the random variable $X \sim N(3, 0.003)$. The length of the bottle, not including the cap, (in centimetres) is given by the random variable $Y \sim N(20, 0.06)$.

What percentage of bottles will not fit on a shelf with a space of 23.5 cm below the next shelf?

3 The thickness in centimetres of an Oatbix is given by a random variable $X \sim N(1.9, 0.01)$. There are twelve Oatbix in a packet. What percentage of boxes that are 24 cm long are too small?

4 A storage cupboard has width X cm, where $X \sim N(79, 1.25)$. What is the probability that five similar cupboards placed side by side will fit along a wall 3.98 m long?

5 The internal diameter (in millimetres) of a nut is a random variable $X \sim N(10, 0.013)$. The diameter (in millimetres) of a bolt is a random variable $Y \sim N(9.5, 0.013)$.

(a) If the difference between the two diameters is less than 0.2 mm, the nut and bolt jam tight. What percentage of nuts and bolts jam?

(b) If the difference between the two diameters is more than 0.75 mm, the nut and bolt are too loose. What percentage of nuts and bolts are too loose?

6 A small saucepan has an external diameter (in centimetres) given by the random variable $X \sim N(18, 0.005)$. The saucepan lid has an internal diameter (in centimetres) given by the random variable $Y \sim N(18.2, 0.005)$.

What percentage of the lids do not fit their saucepans if the gap must not ever be less than 0.05 cm?

After studying this chapter you should:

1 know what probability density means for a continuous random variable;

2 know how to calculate the mean and variance from a probability density function;

3 know how to calculate the probability of an event when given the probability density function of the variable;

4 know and understand that, if $f(x)$ is a probability density function, then:

(a) $f(x) > 0$ for all x;

(b) $\int f(x)\,dx = 1$;

5 be familiar with the uniform, exponential and Normal distributions and the sorts of situation they describe;

6 know how to combine two or more independent Normal variables and know and be able to use the result:

if:

$$X \sim N(\mu_x, \sigma_x^2), \quad Y \sim N(\mu_y, \sigma_y^2)$$

then:

$$X \pm Y \sim N(\mu_x \pm \mu_y, \sigma_x^2 + \sigma_y^2)$$

Combining Normal variables

> You will need:
> • The program *NComb*.

NComb allows you to select variables at random from two Normal distributions X and Y and to combine them by:

• adding $(X + Y)$;

• subtracting $(X - Y)$;

• multiplying by a constant (tX).

The variables are defined as:

$$X \sim N(\mu_x, \sigma_x^2) \qquad Y \sim N(\mu_y, \sigma_y^2)$$

where the values of μ_x, μ_y, σ_x^2 and σ_y^2 are to be input.

1 For the two Normal distributions:

$$X \sim N(10, 1) \quad \text{and} \quad Y \sim N(5, 1)$$

write down:

(a) $E(X + Y)$ (b) $V(X + Y)$

2 Use *NComb* to obtain about 300 values of $X + Y$. The computer will plot the histogram which shows the distribution of the variable $X + Y$. Is it Normal? How can you tell?

3 (a) Using the program, obtain the proportion of observations which are:

  (i) less than the mean value;

  (ii) within one standard deviation of the mean value;

  (iii) within two standard deviations of the mean value;

  (iv) more than three standard deviations from the mean.

(b) Is the distribution of $X + Y$ Normal?

4 Repeat the investigation for other combinations. Try, for example:

(a) $X - Y$ (b) $2X$ (c) $3X$ (d) $2X + Y$

You should be able to write down the mean and variance for each combination. You should also determine whether or not the distribution is approximately Normal.

Solutions

1 Models for data

1.2 Observed and expected frequencies

> Using these assumptions, show that the probability of each of the
> events (boy first, boy second), (boy first, girl second),
> (girl first, girl second) and (girl first, boy second) is 0.25.

If you assume that a baby is equally likely to be a boy or girl and that the sex
of the second child is independent of the first, then the probability of:

$$\text{boy, boy } = \tfrac{1}{2} \times \tfrac{1}{2} = 0.25$$
$$\text{boy, girl } = \tfrac{1}{2} \times \tfrac{1}{2} = 0.25$$
$$\text{girl, boy } = \tfrac{1}{2} \times \tfrac{1}{2} = 0.25$$
$$\text{girl, girl } = \tfrac{1}{2} \times \tfrac{1}{2} = 0.25$$

> Three coins were tossed 800 times and the number of heads recorded.
> The following data were obtained:
>
> | Number of heads | 0 | 1 | 2 | 3 |
> |---|---|---|---|---|
> | Frequency | 78 | 255 | 341 | 126 |
>
> Construct a probability model for this situation and calculate the
> expected frequencies.

A probability model for this situation would assume that:

- each coin was equally likely to come down head or tail;

- each trial is independent.

On this basis, P(no heads in three cases) $= (\tfrac{1}{2})^3 = \tfrac{1}{8}$

In 800 such throws, the expected frequency is $800 \times \tfrac{1}{8} = 100$.

Similarly,

$$P(1 \text{ head}) \;=\; \binom{3}{1}\left(\frac{1}{2}\right)\left(\frac{1}{2}\right)^2 = \frac{3}{8}; \qquad \text{expected frequency} = 300$$

$$P(2 \text{ heads}) \;=\; \binom{3}{2}\left(\frac{1}{2}\right)^2\left(\frac{1}{2}\right) = \frac{3}{8}; \qquad \text{expected frequency} = 300$$

$$P(3 \text{ heads}) \;=\; \left(\frac{1}{2}\right)^3 = \frac{1}{8}; \qquad \text{expected frequency} = 100$$

1.3 How good is the model?

1 (a) (i) With P(boy) = $\frac{1}{2}$ the expected frequencies would be:

	Boy first	Girl first
Boy second	25	25
Girl second	25	25

So $X^2 = \dfrac{(31-25)^2}{25} + \dfrac{(21-25)^2}{25} + \dfrac{(22-25)^2}{25} + \dfrac{(26-25)^2}{25}$

$= 2.48$

(ii) With P(boy) = 0.513 the expected frequencies would be:

	Boy first	Girl first
Boy second	26.3	25
Girl second	25	23.7

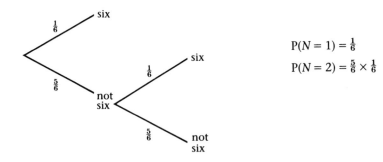

$100 \times P(99) = 100 \times 0.417^2$

$X^2 = \dfrac{(31-26.3)^2}{26.3} + \dfrac{(21-25)^2}{25} + \dfrac{(22-25)^2}{25} + \dfrac{(26-23.7)^2}{23.7}$

$= 2.06$

(b) Model (ii) fits these data better.

2 (a)

First throw   Second throw

six

six

not
six

not
six

$P(N = 1) = \frac{1}{6}$

$P(N = 2) = \frac{5}{6} \times \frac{1}{6}$

(i) $P(N = 1) = \frac{1}{6}$

(ii) $P(N = 2) = \frac{5}{6} \times \frac{1}{6}$

(iii) $P(N = 3) = \frac{5}{6} \times \frac{5}{6} \times \frac{1}{6}$

(b)

N	1	2	3	4	5	6 or more
$P(N = n)$	0.167	0.139	0.116	0.096	0.08	0.402
Expected frequencies	33.4	27.8	23.2	19.2	16	80.4

(c) $X^2 = 4.5$

3 1560 books were loaned.

Expected number loaned per day $= \dfrac{1560}{6} = 260$

$$X^2 = \frac{(200 - 260)^2}{260} + \frac{(290 - 260)^2}{260} + \ldots$$
$$= 20.6$$

2 The chi-squared test

2.1 The distribution of X^2

Find the value 18.55 in the table. Find also:

(a) the value of $\chi^2(12)$ which has 1% of the area to the right;

(b) the value of $\chi^2(5)$ which has 5% of the area to the right.

(a) 26.22   (b) 11.07

Consider the other dice in the same way.

Die B: $X^2 = 0.01$
Here there is almost perfect agreement between the proposed model and the 'real' data. This seems too good to be true!

Die C: $X^2 = 5.43$
The table indicates that a value higher than 4.61 would occur by chance in fewer than 10% of cases. Since the value obtained exceeds this, you might conclude that the difference between the real data and the model of a fair die is too great to have occurred by chance and the die may be biased. Hence the result is significant at the 10% level.

Die D: $X^2 = 10.85$

This is a high value. For a fair die, a value as great or greater than 10.60 (from tables) would occur in only $\frac{1}{2}$% of all cases. This is a highly significant difference and is significant at the 0.5% level. It is likely that this is not a fair die.

EXERCISE 1

1 (a) 2.5%   (b) 5%   (c) 2.5%

2 (a) $a = 18.31$ (b) $b = 2.56$ (c) $c = 20.48$

2.2 Testing a model

Confirm that the probability of one girl in a family of three is $\frac{3}{8}$ and that the expected frequency is 19.13.

$$P(1 \text{ girl}) = \binom{3}{1}\left(\frac{1}{2}\right)\left(\frac{1}{2}\right)^2 = \frac{3}{8}$$

$\binom{3}{1} = 3 \text{ ways}$ $P(1 \text{ girl})$ $P(2 \text{ boys})$

The expected frequency (in 51 families) $= \dfrac{3}{8} \times 51 = 19.13$.

EXERCISE 2

1

Month	Jan	Feb	Mar	Apr	May	Jun	Jul	Aug	Sept	Oct	Nov	Dec
O	30	30	33	42	25	28	41	32	48	28	28	24
E		32.42	32.42	32.42	32.42	32.42	32.42	32.42	32.42	32.42	32.42	32.42	32.42

$X^2 = 18.66$

There are 12 cells giving 11 degrees of freedom.
The result is not significant at the 5% level but is significant at the 10% level. There is some evidence to suggest that assaults do not occur equally throughout the year.

2

Sample	1	2	3	4	5	6
O	40	35	30	30	25	20
E	30	30	30	30	30	30

$X^2 = 8.33$

There are six cells, giving five degrees of freedom.
$\chi^2 < 9.24$ in 90% of samples, so there is insufficient evidence to disprove the hypothesis. The difference is not significant.

3

Pea classification	RY	WY	RG	WG	W = wrinkled
O	55	20	16	9	R = round
E	56.25	18.75	18.75	6.25	Y = yellow
					G = green

$X^2 = 1.72$

There are four cells, giving three degrees of freedom.
$\chi^2 < 6.25$ in 90% of samples, so you can conclude that these results agree with Mendelian theory.

4 The proportion of imperfect peaches is 15%.

Number of imperfect peaches in box	0	1	2	3	4	5	6
Expected frequency	37.71	39.93	17.62	4.15	0.55	0.04	0

Number of imperfect peaches in box	0	1	2	3 or more
O	50	25	14	11
E	37.71	39.93	17.62	4.74

$X^2 = 18.60$ The number of degrees of freedom is three.

$\chi^2(3) > 16.27$ in fewer than 0.1% of samples. The difference is highly significant (at the 0.1% level). The model used does not give a good fit with the data collected.

2.4 Contingency tables

> (a) Why are there three free entries in each column, and four free entries in each row?
>
> (b) For this table, there are $3 \times 4 = 12$ degrees of freedom. How many degrees of freedom are there for an m by n table?

(a) Once three free entries are put in a column the fourth entry is fixed. Similarly, when four entries have been placed in each row, the fifth entry is fixed to give the required total.

(b) In an m by n table there will be $(m - 1) \times (n - 1)$ degrees of freedom.

EXERCISE 3

1 The model used assumes that there is no difference in grades awarded and gives the following table of expected grades.

		Grade			
	1	2	3	4	Total
College A	6.31	60.79	114.69	60.21	242
College B	4.69	45.21	85.31	44.79	180
Total	11	106	200	105	422

$$X^2 = 1.78 \qquad \nu = 3$$

$\chi^2(3) < 6.25$ in 90% of samples.
There is no evidence that there is any significant difference in grades awarded by the two colleges.

2 The proportion of staff who are satisfied overall is $\frac{92}{190}$.
From this, the expected frequencies of all types of staff can be calculated.

	Satisfied	Not satisfied	Total
Doctors	34	36	70
Nurses	29	31	60
Ancillary staff	29	31	60
Total	92	98	190

The initial assumption is that job satisfaction is not related to the job done.

$$X^2 = 34 \qquad \text{The number of degrees of freedom} = (3 - 1)(2 - 1) = 2$$

$\chi^2(2) > 13.82$ in less than 0.1% of samples. The evidence against the initial assumption is very significant, suggesting that job satisfaction is related to job done.

3 An initial assumption that the drug is not effective would give the following expected frequency table:

	Drug	Placebo	Total
Improved	95.5	95.5	191
Not improved	104.5	104.5	209
Total	200	200	400

$X^2 = 22.13$ The number of degrees of freedom = 1

At the 5% level, $\chi^2 = 3.84$. Thus there is significant evidence to disprove the initial assumption and you can conclude that the drug is effective in improving the condition.

3 Probability distributions for counting cases

3.1 Introduction

State the necessary assumptions.

The assumptions are that:

- the probability of a girl is the same for each birth;
- each birth is independent;
- there are no multiple births (for example, twins).

For a general uniform distribution, show that:

$$P(X = r) = \frac{1}{k} \quad \text{for } r = 1, 2, \ldots, k$$

As the distribution is uniform, $P(X = r) = a$, for $r = 1, 2, \ldots, k$, where a is a constant.

However, the total probability is 1 so $\displaystyle\sum_{r=1}^{k} P(X = r) = 1$,

i.e. $\displaystyle\sum_{r=1}^{k} a = 1$, so $ka = 1$ and $a = \dfrac{1}{k}$ as required.

3.2 The geometric distribution

X can never equal 0. Why not?

The smallest value of X occurs when the event occurs on the first trial, i.e. when $X = 1$.

EXERCISE 1

1 (a) $P(X = 3) = (0.8)^2(0.2) = 0.128$

(b) $P(X < 3) = P(X = 1) + P(X = 2)$
$$= 0.2 + (0.8)(0.2) = 0.36$$

(c) $P(X \geqslant 3) = 1 - P(X < 3) = 0.64$

2 Let X denote the number of trials before selecting the right key.

(a) (i) $P(X = 2) = \frac{3}{4} \times \frac{1}{3} = \frac{1}{4}$

(ii) $P(X = 4) = \frac{3}{4} \times \frac{2}{3} \times \frac{1}{2} = \frac{1}{4}$

(b) $X \sim G\left(\frac{1}{4}\right)$

(i) $P(X = 2) = \frac{3}{4} \times \frac{1}{4} = \frac{3}{16}$

(ii) $P(X > 2) = 1 - (P(X = 1) + P(X = 2))$
$$= 1 - \left(\frac{1}{4} + \frac{3}{16}\right) = \frac{9}{16}$$

(c) The first strategy is the best as it guarantees finding the correct key within 4 trials. Also, the first strategy has a higher probability for 2, 3 and 4 trials than the second strategy.

3 (a) Let X denote the number of attempts required to pass.
Then $X \sim G(0.4)$
$$P(X = 3) = (0.6)^2(0.4) = 0.144$$

(b) $P(X > 5) = 1 - P(X \leqslant 5)$
$$= 1 - [P(X = 1) + P(X = 2) + P(X = 3) + P(X = 4) + P(X = 5)]$$
$$= 1 - [0.4 + (0.4)(0.6) + (0.4)(0.6)^2 + (0.4)(0.6)^3$$
$$+ (0.4)(0.6)^4]$$
$$= 1 - 0.9224 = 0.0776$$

4 (a) $\left(\frac{9}{10}\right)^5 = 0.59049$
$$= 0.59 \quad \text{(to 2 s.f.)}$$

(b) Having to select more than 20 to obtain the first zero means that all of the first 20 digits are non-zero.
$$P(20 \text{ non-zero digits}) = \left(\frac{9}{10}\right)^{20}$$
$$= 0.122$$

3.3 The binomial distribution revisited

Use the factorial form of the binomial distribution to find the probability of there being only one male baby in a group of ten.

If X is the number of boys in the ward, then

$$X \sim B(10, \tfrac{1}{2})$$

$$P(X = 1) = \binom{10}{1}\left(\frac{1}{2}\right)\left(\frac{1}{2}\right)^9 = \frac{10!}{9!1!}\left(\frac{1}{2}\right)^{10}$$

$$= 10(0.5)^{10} = 0.0098 \quad \text{(to 2 s.f.)}$$

EXERCISE 2

1   X denotes the number of times the team won the toss.

$$X \sim B(5, 0.5)$$

(a) $P(X = 3) = \binom{5}{3}(0.5)^2(0.5)^3$

$$= \frac{5!}{3!2!}(0.5)^5 = 0.3125$$

(b) $P(X \geqslant 3)$ $\quad = P(X = 3) + P(X = 4) + P(X = 5)$

$P(X = 4)$ $\quad = \binom{5}{4}(0.5)^5 = 5(0.5)^5 = 0.15625$

$P(X = 5)$ $\quad = \binom{5}{5}(0.5)^5 = 0.03125$

$\Rightarrow P(X \geqslant 3) = 0.3125 + 0.15625 + 0.03125 = 0.5$

[This result could have been obtained by symmetry.]

2   $X \sim B(8, \tfrac{2}{3})$

$$P(X = 0) = \left(\frac{1}{3}\right)^8 = 0.00015$$

$$P(X = 1) = \binom{8}{1}\left(\frac{2}{3}\right)\left(\frac{1}{3}\right)^7 = 0.00244$$

$$P(X = 2) = \binom{8}{2}\left(\frac{2}{3}\right)^2\left(\frac{1}{3}\right)^6 = 0.01707$$

$$P(X = 3) = \binom{8}{3}\left(\frac{2}{3}\right)^3\left(\frac{1}{3}\right)^5 = 0.06828$$

$$P(X=4) = \binom{8}{4}\left(\frac{2}{3}\right)^4\left(\frac{1}{3}\right)^4 = 0.17071$$

$$P(X=5) = \binom{8}{5}\left(\frac{2}{3}\right)^5\left(\frac{1}{3}\right)^3 = 0.27313$$

$$P(X=6) = \binom{8}{6}\left(\frac{2}{3}\right)^6\left(\frac{1}{3}\right)^2 = 0.27313$$

$$P(X=7) = \binom{8}{7}\left(\frac{2}{3}\right)^7\left(\frac{1}{3}\right) = 0.15607$$

$$P(X=8) = \left(\frac{2}{3}\right)^8 = 0.03902$$

So 5 and 6 are the values which are most likely to occur.

3 You can approach this question by seeing how likely the outcome is if there is no preference for A or B.

Let X denote the number of people who prefer brand B. Then $X \sim B(6, 0.5)$.

$$P(X=5) = \binom{6}{5}(0.5)(0.5)^5 = 6(0.5)^6 = 0.09375 \text{ i.e. almost 1 in 10}$$

In practice this would not be considered to be sufficiently small to discard the assumption that A and B are equally well-liked.

4 Let X denote the number of correct questions. Then $X \sim B(20, \frac{1}{3})$.

$$\begin{aligned} P(X \geqslant 15) &= P(X=15) + P(X=16) + P(X=17) + P(X=18) \\ &\quad + P(X=19) + P(X=20) \end{aligned}$$

$$= \binom{20}{15}\left(\frac{1}{3}\right)^{15}\left(\frac{2}{3}\right)^5 + \binom{20}{16}\left(\frac{1}{3}\right)^{16}\left(\frac{2}{3}\right)^4 + \binom{20}{17}\left(\frac{1}{3}\right)^{17}\left(\frac{2}{3}\right)^3 + \dots$$

$$= 0.000167 \quad \text{(to 3 s.f.)}$$

5E P(same number of heads on first 4 throws as last 4)

$$\begin{aligned} &= P(X=0, Y=0) + P(X=1, Y=1) + P(X=2, Y=2) + P(X=3, Y=3) \\ &\quad + P(X=4, Y=4) \text{ where } X \text{ and } Y \text{ denote the number of heads on the} \\ &\quad \text{first and last 4 throws respectively} \end{aligned}$$

$$= \left[(0.5)^4\right]^2 + \left[4(0.5)^4\right]^2 + \left[\binom{4}{2}(0.5)^4\right]^2 + \left[\binom{4}{3}(0.5)^4\right]^2 + \left[(0.5)^4\right]^2$$

$$= 0.273$$

By symmetry, the probability that there are more tails on the first four throws than the last four $= \dfrac{1 - 0.273}{2} = 0.36 \quad \text{(to 2 s.f.)}$

3.4   The Poisson distribution

EXERCISE 3

1   (a) $P(0) = e^{-1.4} = 0.247$ (to 3 s.f.)

   (b) $P(2 \text{ or more}) = 1 - P(0) - P(1)$
                   $P(1) = 1.4\,e^{-1.4}$
          $\Rightarrow P(2 \text{ or more}) = 0.408$ (to 3 s.f.)

2   (a) 2

   (b)   (i) $P(0) = \begin{pmatrix} 100 \\ 0 \end{pmatrix}(0.02)^0(0.98)^{100} = (0.98)^{100} = 0.133$ (to 3 s.f.)

          (ii) $P(\text{at least one}) = 1 - P(0) = 0.867$ (to 3 s.f.)

   (c) $\mu = np = 2$
          $P(0) = e^{-2} = 0.135$ (to 3 s.f.)
          $P(\text{at least one}) = 1 - 0.135 = 0.865$ (to 3 s.f.)

3   (a) $P(X = 0) = \dfrac{e^{-5}5^0}{0!} = e^{-5} = 0.00674$

   (b) $P(X = 2) = \dfrac{e^{-5}5^2}{2!} = 0.0842$

   (c) $P(X \geqslant 2) = 1 - P(X = 0 \text{ or } 1)$
                       $= 1 - (e^{-5} + 5e^{-5})$
                       $= 0.960$ (to 3 s.f.)

4   Let X be the number of customers arriving at the check-out.

          $X \sim P(\lambda = 2.4)$

       $P(X > 3) = 1 - P(X = 0, 1, 2 \text{ or } 3)$

$$= 1 - \left[e^{-2.4} + 2.4\,e^{-2.4} + \frac{2.4^2 e^{-2.4}}{2} + \frac{2.4^3 e^{-2.4}}{3!} \right]$$

$$= 1 - e^{-2.4}\left(1 + 2.4 + \frac{2.4^2}{2} + \frac{2.4^3}{6} \right)$$

$$= 1 - 0.779$$
$$= 0.221 \quad \text{(to 3 s.f.)}$$

4 Selecting and testing the models

4.1 Choosing a suitable model

> For each variable, suggest whether the binomial, Poisson or geometric are likely to be suitable models. State assumptions you need to make and define the model where possible.
>
> (a) The number of sixes obtained when five dice are thrown.
>
> (b) The number of throws needed before you obtain a six on a die.
>
> (c) The number of boys in families of four children.
>
> (d) The number of clicks made by a geiger counter in a five-second interval.
>
> (e) The number of home matches a team plays before they score a goal.

(a) Binomial. Assume each die is independent.

$$X \sim B(5, \tfrac{1}{6})$$

(b) Geometric. Assume independence.

$$X \sim G(\tfrac{1}{6})$$

(c) Binomial. Assume births are independent.

$X \sim B(4, 0.5)$ or $X \sim B(4, 0.513)$, assuming that P(boy) = 0.513 as stated in tasksheet 1 of chapter 3.

(d) Poisson. Assume radioactive emissions occur randomly, singly and independently. λ would be defined as the average number of emissions in a five-second interval.

(e) Geometric. To specify the model in further detail you need to know the probability of a goal being scored in a home match.

EXERCISE 1

1 (a) The binomial distribution is a possible model as each event has two possible outcomes (boy or girl) and births can be regarded as being independent. If it is assumed that boys and girls are equally likely outcomes, then $p = \tfrac{1}{2}$. As there are five children in each family, $n = 5$.

(b)

		Expected Values
$P(X = 0) =$	$(\frac{1}{2})^5 = 0.03125$	$300 \times P(X = 0) = 9.375$
$P(X = 1) =$	$5(\frac{1}{2})^5 = 0.15625$	$300 \times P(X = 1) = 46.875$
$P(X = 2) =$	$10(\frac{1}{2})^5 = 0.3125$	$300 \times P(X = 2) = 93.75$
$P(X = 3) =$	$10(\frac{1}{2})^5 = 0.3125$	$300 \times P(X = 3) = 93.75$
$P(X = 4) =$	$5(\frac{1}{2})^5 = 0.15625$	$300 \times P(X = 4) = 46.875$
$P(X = 5) =$	$(\frac{1}{2})^5 = 0.03125$	$300 \times P(X = 5) = 9.375$

$$X^2 = \sum \frac{(O - E)^2}{E} = 11.04$$

There are six cells and therefore five degrees of freedom.
$\chi^2(5) = 11.07$ at the 5% level
So there is insufficient evidence to reject the model.

(c) Number of boys   = 809
Number of children = 1500

$$\text{So } p = \frac{809}{1500}$$

			Expected values
$P(X = 0) = q^5 (q = 1 - p)$		$= 0.021$	6.22
$P(X = 1) = 5pq^4$		$= 0.121$	36.43
$P(X = 2) = 10p^2 q^3$		$= 0.284$	85.31
$P(X = 3) = 10p^3 q^2$		$= 0.333$	99.88
$P(X = 4) = 15p^4 q$		$= 0.195$	58.47
$P(X = 5) = p^5$		$= 0.046$	13.69

$$X^2 = \sum \frac{(O - E)^2}{E} = 1.135$$

$\chi^2(4) = 9.49$ at the 5% level

The fit appears to be much better.
Note that there are only four degrees of freedom as there are two constraints, the probability and the total.

(d) The second model gives the best fit. You would expect this as p is estimated from the data.

2E (a) *N* has a binomial distribution as it has only two possible outcomes (point up or down) and you can assume that each drawing pin lands independently of the others.

(b) (i) Number of pins landing point up = 690
Number of trials = 1200

So an estimate of *p* is $\frac{690}{1200} = 0.575$

(ii) Assume $N \sim B(4, p)$.

		Expected values
$P(N = 0) = (1 - p)^4$	$= 0.032$	9.79
$P(N = 1) = 4p(1 - p)^3$	$= 0.177$	52.97
$P(N = 2) = 6p^2(1 - p)^2$	$= 0.358$	107.49
$P(N = 3) = 4p^3(1 - p)$	$= 0.323$	96.96
$P(N = 4) = p^4$	$= 0.109$	32.79

$$\chi^2 = \sum \frac{(O - E)^2}{E} = 3.5$$

There are three degrees of freedom (5 cells − 2 constraints).
$\chi^2 = 7.81$
So the model is suitable.

4.2 The geometric distribution as a model

> The data show that the player scored 44 baskets out of 126 shots. How is this worked out?

44 baskets is the total frequency.
126 shots is calculated from $1 \times 10 + 2 \times 11 + 3 \times 9 + \ldots + 8 \times 1$.

> Show that $X^2 = 6.2$ (to 2 s.f.).

This is obtained from calculating $\dfrac{(10 - 15.4)^2}{15.4} + \dfrac{(11 - 10)^2}{10} + \ldots + \dfrac{(3 - 5.2)^2}{5.2}$

> What are the two constraints?

One constraint is the value of *p*. The other is that the total number of baskets must be 44.

4.3 Fitting a Poisson distribution to data

EXERCISE 2

1 (a) $\bar{x} = \text{mean} = \dfrac{81}{60} = 1.35$

Variance $= \dfrac{1}{n}\left(\sum x^2\right) - \bar{x}^2 = 1.19$ (to 3 s.f.)

(b) You can consider the arrival of customers as random and independent and the variance as close to the mean.

2 (a) As the disease is not known to be infectious, you can assume that its outbreak is random and independent. Since the values of the mean, 1.26, and variance, 1.57, are reasonably close, a Poisson model is reasonable.

(b)

X	0	1	2	3	4	5	6	7
P(X)	0.28	0.36	0.23	0.09	0.03	0.008	0.002	0.0003
E	28.4	35.7	22.5	9.46	2.98	0.75	0.16	0.028

13.38

Group these cells together to make the expected frequency greater than 5.

(c) $\sum \dfrac{(O - E)^2}{E} = 0.341$

There are now four cells and two constraints, giving $4 - 2 = 2$ degrees of freedom.

$\chi^2(2) = 5.99$ (at the 5% level)

The model is a good fit.

3 (a) $\lambda = \dfrac{196}{280} = 0.7$ (b)

	E
$P(X = 0) = 0.497$	139.0
$P(X = 1) = 0.348$	97.3
$P(X = 2) = 0.122$	34.1
$P(X = 3) = 0.028$	7.95 ⎫
$P(X = 4) = 0.005$	1.39 ⎬ 9.53
$P(X = 5) = 0.0007$	0.19 ⎭

(c) The fit appears to be reasonable.

(d) $\sum \dfrac{(O - E)^2}{E} = 1.98$

There are four cells with two constraints, so there are two degrees of freedom.

$\chi^2(2) = 5.99$ (at the 5% level) suggesting that the model is satisfactory

5 Forming new variables

5.1 Games of chance

> Use these ideas and results to analyse the dice game described at the beginning of this chapter.

Score on die (D)	1	2	3	4	5	6
Probability	$\frac{1}{6}$	$\frac{1}{6}$	$\frac{1}{6}$	$\frac{1}{6}$	$\frac{1}{6}$	$\frac{1}{6}$

Mean (D) $= \frac{1}{6}(1 + 2 + 3 + 4 + 5 + 6)$
$= 3.5$
Variance $(D) = \frac{1}{6}(1^2 + 2^2 + 3^2 + 4^2 + 5^2 + 6^2) - (3.5)^2$
≈ 2.9

Option 1:
Mean $(D_1 + D_2)$ $= 2$ mean $(D) = 7$
Variance $(D_1 + D_2) =$ variance $(D) +$ variance (D)
$= 2$ variance $(D) \approx 5.8$

Option 2:
Mean $(2D)$ $= 2$ mean $(D) = 7$
Variance $(2D) = 2^2$ variance (D)
$= 4$ variance $(D) \approx 11.7$

The expected winnings are the same for each option. Your prize money would be 7p minus the cost to play. If it cost less than 7p per go, then you would expect (in the long term) to win on both options.

The variance (variability) is much greater with option 2. You have a chance of winning (or losing) more per go.

More cautious players might prefer option 1!

EXERCISE 1

1

x	1	2	5	8
$P(X = x)$	$\frac{1}{4}$	$\frac{1}{4}$	$\frac{1}{4}$	$\frac{1}{4}$

(a) (i) $\text{Mean}(X) = (1 \times \frac{1}{4}) + (2 \times \frac{1}{4}) + (5 \times \frac{1}{4}) + (8 \times \frac{1}{4})$
$= \frac{1}{4} \times 16 = 4$

(ii) $\text{Variance}(X) = (1^2 \times \frac{1}{4}) + (2^2 \times \frac{1}{4}) + (5^2 \times \frac{1}{4}) + (8^2 \times \frac{1}{4}) - 4^2$
$= \frac{1}{4}(1 + 4 + 25 + 64) - 16$
$= \frac{94}{4} - 16 = 7.5$

(b) $\text{Mean}(2X) = 2\,\text{mean}(X) = 2 \times 4 = 8$
Variance $= V(2X) = 4V(X) = 4 \times 7.5 = 30$

(c) $\text{Mean}(3X) = 3\,\text{mean}(X) = 3 \times 4 = 12$
Variance $= V(3X) = 9V(X) = 9 \times 7.5 = 67.5$

(d) $\text{Mean}(X_1 + X_2) = \text{mean}(X_1) + \text{mean}(X_2)$
$= 2\,\text{mean}(X) = 8.0$
$\text{Variance}(X_1 + X_2) = V(X_1) + V(X_2)$
$= 2\,V(X) = 15.0$

2

x	1	2	3	4
$P(X = x)$	$\frac{1}{6}$	$\frac{2}{6}$	$\frac{2}{6}$	$\frac{1}{6}$

(a) Mean $= (1 \times \frac{1}{6}) + (2 \times \frac{2}{6}) + (3 \times \frac{2}{6}) + (4 \times \frac{1}{6})$
$= \frac{1}{6}(1 + 4 + 6 + 4) = \frac{15}{6} = 2.5$
Variance $= (1^2 \times \frac{1}{6}) + (2^2 \times \frac{2}{6}) + (3^2 \times \frac{2}{6}) + (4^2 \times \frac{1}{6}) - 2.5^2$
$= \frac{1}{6}(1 + 8 + 18 + 16) - 6.25 = \frac{43}{6} - 6.25 = 7\frac{1}{6} - 6\frac{1}{4}$
≈ 0.917

(b) $\text{Mean}(2X) = 2\,\text{mean}(X) = 5$
$\text{Variance}(2X) = 4V(X) \approx 3.7$

(c) $\text{Mean}(X_1 + 2X_2) = \text{mean}(X) + 2\,\text{mean}(X) = 7.5$
$\text{Variance}(X_1 + 2X_2) = V(X) + 4V(X) \approx 4.6$

5.3 Combining Poisson variables

EXERCISE 2

1 (a) Mean $(A + B) = \mu_A + \mu_B$
   Variance $(A + B) = \sigma_A^2 + \sigma_B^2$

(b) Mean $(2A) = 2\mu_A$
   Variance $(2A) = 4\sigma_A^2$

(c) Mean $(3A - B) = 3\mu_A - \mu_B$
   Variance$(3A - B) = 9\sigma_A^2 + \sigma_B^2$

2 (a) Mean$(X + Y) = $ mean$(X) + $ mean(Y)
   $= 4 + 3 = 7$

(b) $X + Y \sim P(\lambda) = 7$
   $P(X + Y < 4) = P(X + Y = 0, 1, 2 \text{ or } 3)$
   $$= e^{-7} + 7e^{-7} + \frac{7^2 e^{-7}}{2!} + \frac{7^3 e^{-7}}{3!}$$

   $$= e^{-7}\left(1 + 7 + \frac{49}{2!} + \frac{343}{3!}\right)$$

   $$= 0.0818$$

3 (a) $X \sim P(3)$ mean$(X) = 3$ variance$(X) = 3$
   $Y \sim P(2)$ mean$(Y) = 2$ variance$(Y) = 2$
   mean$(X + Y) = 3 + 2 = 5$
   variance$(X + Y) = 3 + 2 = 5$

(b) $X + Y \sim P(\lambda = 5)$

   (i) P(no calls) $= e^{-5} = 0.00674$

   (ii) P(more than 2 calls) $= 1 - P(0, 1 \text{ or } 2 \text{ calls})$
   $$= 1 - \left(e^{-5} + 5e^{-5} + \frac{5^2 e^{-5}}{2!}\right)$$
   $$= 0.875$$

5.4 Expectation

> Find $E[2X^2]$

$E[2X^2] = 2(1^2 \times 0.2 + 2^2 \times 0.8)$
$= 2(0.2 + 3.2) = 6.8$

> Show that:
>
> (a) $E[aX] = aE[X]$
>
> (b) $V[aX] = a^2 V[X]$

(a) $E[aX] = \sum ax_iP(x_i) = a\sum x_iP(x_i) = aE[X]$

(b) $V[aX] = E[a^2X^2] - (E[aX])^2$
$\quad\quad\quad = a^2E[X^2] - a^2(E[X])^2$
$\quad\quad\quad = a^2\{E[X^2] - (E[x])^2\}$
$\quad\quad\quad = a^2V[X]$

5.5 The mean and variance of B(*n*, *p*) – a proof

> Show that the mean and variance of X are p and pq respectively.

$E[X] = 0 \times q + 1 \times p = p$
$V[X] = E[X^2] - (E[X])^2$
$\quad\quad = 0^2 \times q + 1^2 \times p - p^2$
$\quad\quad = p - p^2$
$\quad\quad = p(1 - p)$
$\quad\quad = pq, \quad \text{since } q = 1 - p$

> In the argument given above, explain why lines ① and ② are correct.

Line ① uses the result $E(X_1 + X_2) = E(X_1) + E(X_2)$ proved earlier.
Line ② use the fact that X_i has the same probability distribution as X.

6 Continuous random variables

6.1 The Normal probability density function

EXERCISE 1

1   Let the total journey time be T minutes.

$\quad\quad T \sim N(20, 5^2)$

$P(T > 26)$ is required.

Standardising, $z = \dfrac{26 - 20}{5} = 1.2$

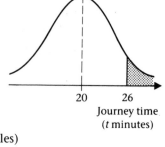

$P(T > 26) \quad = 1 - \Phi(1.2)$
$\quad\quad\quad\quad\quad\quad = 1 - 0.885 \quad \text{(from tables)}$
$\quad\quad\quad\quad\quad\quad = 0.115$

I will be late on about 12% of journeys.

2 Let the lifetime of a bulb be t hours.

$$T \sim N(2000, 50^2)$$

(a) $P(T > 1970)$

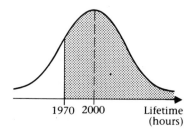

$$\frac{1970 - 2000}{50} = -0.6$$

$$
\begin{aligned}
P(T > 1970) &= 1 - \Phi(-0.6) \\
&= 1 - [1 - \Phi(0.6)] \\
&= \Phi(0.6) \\
&= 0.726
\end{aligned}
$$

(b) $P(2050 < T < 2080)$

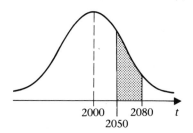

$$\frac{2080 - 2000}{50} = 1.6$$

$$\frac{2050 - 2000}{50} = 1.0$$

$$
\begin{aligned}
\text{Required area} &= \Phi(1.6) - \Phi(1.0) \\
&= 0.945 - 0.841 \\
&= 0.104
\end{aligned}
$$

3 Let the survival time be T days.

$$T \sim N(20, \sigma^2)$$

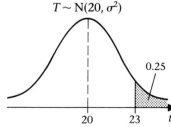

$$\Phi(z) = 0.75$$
$$\Rightarrow z = 0.68$$

$$\text{So } \frac{23 - 20}{\sigma} = 0.68$$

$$\sigma = 4.4$$

The standard deviation is about 4.4 days.

6.2 General probability density functions

> Explain why f(x) must have these properties.

$f(x) \geqslant 0$ for all x because $f(x)$ represents a probability which **must** always be greater than or equal to 0 (and less than or equal to 1).

The total area under the graph of $f(x)$, $\displaystyle\int_{-\infty}^{\infty} f(x)\, dx$, represents the probability that one of the X values has occurred. Since the probability is 1 that a value will occur, $\displaystyle\int_{-\infty}^{\infty} f(x)\, dx$ **must** equal 1.

> Write down:
>
> (a) $P(X \geqslant 6)$ (b) $P(X \leqslant 0)$

X can only take values from 0 to 6 inclusive, so $P(X \geqslant 6)$ and $P(X \leqslant 0)$ are zero.

> What is the probability of becoming infected on the first day?

$$P(\text{infected on 1st day}) = \int_0^1 f(x) \, dx$$

$$= \tfrac{1}{144} \left[36x - \tfrac{1}{3}x^3 \right]_0^1$$

$$= \tfrac{1}{144} \left[35\tfrac{2}{3} \right] = 0.25 \quad \text{(to 2 s.f.)}$$

EXERCISE 2

1 (a) $0 \leqslant X \leqslant 3$ (b)

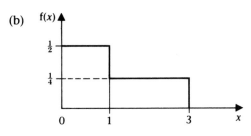

Area under $f(x) = 1 \times \tfrac{1}{2} + 2 \times \tfrac{1}{4} = 1$

(c)   (i) $P(X \geqslant 1)$ $= \tfrac{1}{2}$
    (ii) $P(X \geqslant \tfrac{1}{2})$ $= \tfrac{3}{4}$
    (iii) $P(\tfrac{1}{2} \leqslant X \leqslant 2) = \tfrac{1}{2}$
    (iv) $P(X \leqslant 3)$ $= 1$

2 (a) The area under the curve must equal 1.
Area of triangle $= \tfrac{1}{2}$ base $\times$ height
$$= \tfrac{1}{2} \times 2 \times k = k$$
$$\Rightarrow k = 1$$

(b)   (i) $P(X \geqslant 1.5) = 0.125$

    (ii) $P(X < 0.5) = 0.125$

    (iii) $P(0.5 < X < 1.5) = 0.75$

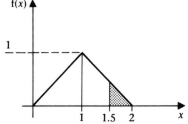

106

3 $0 \leqslant X \leqslant 10$ and $f(x) = 0.0012x^2(10 - x)$

(a) $P(X > 5) = \int_5^{10} f(x)\,dx = 0.0012 \int_5^{10} x^2(10 - x)\,dx$

$$= 0.0012 \left[\tfrac{10}{3}x^3 - \tfrac{1}{4}x^4 \right]_5^{10}$$

$$= 0.0012[(833.3) - (260.4)]$$

$$= 0.687 \quad \text{(to 3 s.f.)}$$

(b) $P(1 < X < 2) = \int_1^2 f(x)\,dx = 0.0012 \left[\tfrac{10}{3}x^3 - \tfrac{1}{4}x^4 \right]_1^2$

$$= 0.0235$$

6.3 The mean and variance

EXERCISE 3

1 (a) $1 = \int_0^1 kx^2\,dx$

$$= k \left[\tfrac{1}{3}x^3 \right]_0^1 = k(\tfrac{1}{3} - 0)$$

$$\Rightarrow k = 3$$

(b) $\mu = \int_0^1 xf(x)\,dx$

$$= 3 \int_0^1 x^3\,dx$$

$$= 3 \left[\tfrac{1}{4}x^4 \right]_0^1$$

$$= 3 \left[(\tfrac{1}{4}) - (0) \right] = \tfrac{3}{4}$$

$$\sigma^2 = E(X^2) - \mu^2$$

$$E(X^2) = 3 \int_0^1 x^2 f(x)\,dx$$

$$= 3 \int_0^1 x^2 x^2\,dx$$

$$= 3 \left[\tfrac{1}{5}x^5 \right]_0^1 = \tfrac{3}{5}$$

$$\Rightarrow \sigma^2 = \tfrac{3}{5} - (\tfrac{3}{4})^2 = 0.0375$$

(c)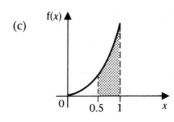

$$P(X \geqslant 0.5) = 3 \int_{0.5}^{1} x^2 \, dx$$

$$= 3 \left[\tfrac{1}{3}x^3 \right]_{0.5}^{1}$$

$$= 1 - 0.5^3 = 0.875$$

2 (a) $\int_{5}^{15} \dfrac{k}{x^3} \, dx = 1$

$\Rightarrow k = 56.25$

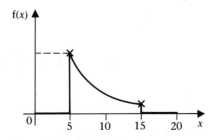

(b)
$$\mu = \int_{5}^{15} x f(x) \, dx$$

$$= k \int_{5}^{15} \frac{x}{x^3} \, dx$$

$$= k \int_{5}^{15} \frac{1}{x^2} \, dx$$

$$= k \left[-\frac{1}{x} \right]_{5}^{15}$$

$$= k((-\tfrac{1}{15}) - (-\tfrac{1}{5}))$$

$$= \tfrac{2}{15}k$$

$$\Rightarrow \mu = 7.5$$

(c)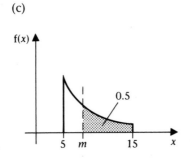

$$0.5 = P(X > m)$$

$$= k \int_{m}^{15} \frac{1}{x^3} \, dx$$

$$= k \left[-\frac{1}{2x^2} \right]_{m}^{15}$$

$$= \frac{k}{2} \left[\left(-\frac{1}{15^2} \right) - \left(-\frac{1}{m^2} \right) \right]$$

$$\Rightarrow m^2 = 45$$

$$\Rightarrow m = 6.71$$

3 $\mu = \displaystyle\int_0^{10} x f(x)\,\mathrm{d}x$

$\quad = 0.0012 \displaystyle\int_0^{10} x^3(10 - x)\,\mathrm{d}x$

$\quad = 0.0012 \displaystyle\int_0^{10} (10x^3 - x^4)\,\mathrm{d}x$

$\quad = 0.0012 \left[\tfrac{10}{4} x^4 - \tfrac{1}{5}x^5 \right]_0^{10}$

$\Rightarrow \mu = 6$

The distance travelled is 6 metres.

6.4 The uniform distribution

> Explain why the height of the rectangle is $\dfrac{1}{b-a}$.

The area must be 1. So, if the height is h then $(b - a)h = 1$, so $h = \dfrac{1}{(b-a)}$.

> A random variable, X, is distributed uniformly and can take any value between 2 and 4.
>
> Find the mean and variance of X.

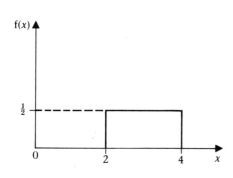

$$f(x) = \begin{cases} \tfrac{1}{2} \text{ for } 2 \leqslant x \leqslant 4 \\ 0 \text{ otherwise} \end{cases}$$

$E(X) = 3 \quad$ by symmetry

$E(X^2) = \displaystyle\int_2^4 x^2 f(x)\,\mathrm{d}x \ = \tfrac{1}{2}\displaystyle\int_2^4 x^2\,\mathrm{d}x$

$\qquad\qquad = \tfrac{1}{2}\left[\tfrac{1}{3}x^3 \right]_2^4 = 9.33$

$V(X) = 9.33 - 9 = 0.33$

109

6.5 The exponential distribution

> Sketch f(x) with λ = 2.
>
> Explain why the probability density is greatest for small values of x.

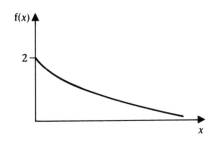

For an initial occurrence in any time interval there must have been no occurrences in earlier intervals. The multiplication of probabilities means that the probabilities associated with later intervals are always smaller.

EXERCISE 4

1 (a)

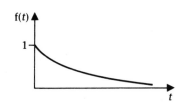

(b) (i)   (ii)

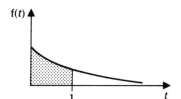   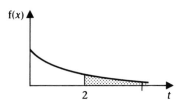

(c) (i) $P(T < 1) = \int_0^1 f(t)\, dt$

$$= \int_0^1 e^{-t}\, dt$$

$$= \left[-1e^{-t} \right]_0^1$$

$$= 0.632$$

(ii) $P(T > 2) = \int_2^\infty e^{-t}\, dt$

$$= \left[-e^{-t} \right]_2^\infty$$

$$P(T > 2) = e^{-2}$$
$$= 0.135$$

2 (a) P(arrival in 1st minute) $= 2 \int_0^1 e^{-2t} \, dt$

$$= 2 \left[\frac{e^{-2t}}{-2} \right]_0^1 = 0.865$$

(b) $2 \int_1^2 e^{-2t} \, dt = 2 \left[\frac{e^{-2t}}{-2} \right]_1^2 = 0.117$

6.6 Combining Normal random variables

EXERCISE 5

1 $X \sim N(14, 0.02)$ $\qquad Y \sim N(9, 0.01)$
Let the total length be L.
$L = X + Y \sim N(23, 0.03)$

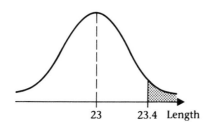

Standardising, $z = \dfrac{23.4 - 23}{\sqrt{(0.03)}} = 2.31$

$P(L > 23.4) = 1 - \Phi(2.31)$
$\qquad\qquad = 0.01044$

23   23.4   Length

2 $X \sim N(3, 0.003)$ $\qquad Y \sim N(20, 0.06)$
Let the total length of the cap plus bottle be L.
$L = X + Y \sim N(23, 0.063)$

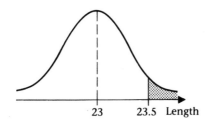

Standardising, $z = \dfrac{23.5 - 23}{\sqrt{(0.063)}} = 1.99$

$P(L > 23.5) = \Phi(1.99)$
$\qquad\qquad = 1 - 0.02330$

2.33% will not fit on the shelf.

23   23.5   Length

3 $X \sim N(1.9, 0.01)$ $\qquad X + X + \ldots \sim N(12 \times 1.9, 12 \times 0.01) = N(22.8, 0.12)$

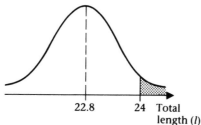

Standardising, $z = \dfrac{24 - 22.8}{\sqrt{(0.12)}} = 3.46$

$P(L > 24) = 1 - \Phi(3.46)$
$\qquad\qquad = 0.00027$

0.027% of boxes are too small.

22.8   24   Total
                length (*l*)

4 $X \sim N(79, 1.25)$ $X + X + \ldots \sim N(5 \times 79, 5 \times 1.25)$
$\sim N(395, 6.25)$

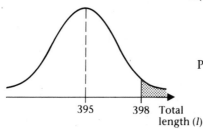

$$z = \frac{398 - 395}{\sqrt{(6.25)}} = 1.20$$
$$P(L \leqslant 398) = \Phi(1.20)$$
$$= 0.885$$

395   398 Total
                 length (l)

5 $X \sim N(10, 0.013)$ $Y \sim N(9.5, 0.013)$
$X - Y \sim N(0.5, 0.026)$

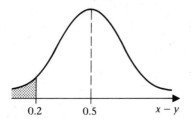

(a) Standardising, $z = \dfrac{0.2 - 0.5}{\sqrt{(0.026)}} = -1.86$
$$P(X - Y < 0.2) = \Phi(-1.86)$$
$$= 1 - \Phi(1.86)$$
$$= 0.03144$$

3.144% of bolts jam.

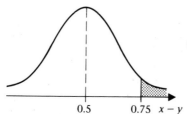

(b) Standardising, $z = \dfrac{0.75 - 0.5}{\sqrt{(0.026)}} = 1.55$
$$P(X - Y > 0.75) = 1 - \Phi(1.55)$$
$$= 0.06057$$

6.057% of bolts are too loose.

6 $X \sim N(18, 0.005)$ $Y \sim N(18.2, 0.005)$
$Y - X \sim N(0.2, 0.01)$

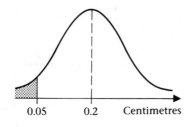

Standardising, $z = \dfrac{0.05 - 0.2}{\sqrt{(0.01)}} = -1.5$
$$P(\text{gap} < 0.05) = \Phi(-1.5)$$
$$= 1 - \Phi(1.5)$$
$$= 0.06681$$

6.681% of lids do not fit.